*Living Salty and Light-filled Lives
in the Workplace*

Living Salty
and Light-filled Lives
in the Workplace

Second Edition

LUKE BOBO

FOREWORD BY JERRAM BARRS

RESOURCE *Publications* · Eugene, Oregon

LIVING SALTY AND LIGHT-FILLED LIVES IN THE WORKPLACE
Second Edition

Resource Publiations
An Imprint of Wipf and Stock Publishers
199 W. 8th Ave., Suite 3
Eugene, OR 97401

www.wipfandstock.com

PAPERBACK ISBN: 978-1-5326-1705-8
HARDCOVER ISBN: 978-1-4982-4143-4
EBOOK ISBN: 978-1-4982-4142-7

Manufactured in the U.S.A.   07/06/2017

This book is dedicated to my supportive,
beautiful, and brilliant wife,
Rita

and my pint-size or diminutive grandmother,
Willa Mae Bobo (1925–2008).

". . . there is no God like you in heaven above or on earth beneath, keeping covenant and showing steadfast love to your servants who walk before you with all their heart."

—1 KINGS 8:23.

Contents

Acknowledgments

I am grateful for and indebted to my wife, Rita, who added *specificity* to this work. One bright sunny morning while sitting at our kitchen table, I proudly announced, "I am going to write a book on being salt and light." And Rita employed her over 20 years of professional marketing experience and said, why not write a book on "being salt and light in the *workplace*." And the rest they say is history!

I am particularly appreciative for my unwed teenage mother who after giving birth to two boys (my brother and I) dropped out of high school to care for us. Although her dream of being an elementary teacher had to be abandoned, she constantly emphasized the virtues of education to us. And I am deeply grateful and indebted to my grandparents, Henry and Willa Mae Bobo, who were not only surrogate parents to me but strongly encouraged me to attend college.

I am also so thankful for these fellow servants in the ministry: Rev. Leo Barbee, who led me to Christ while an engineering student at the University of Kansas (Lawrence, KS); Rev. Dr. Ronald L. Bobo, Sr., who is considered my 'spiritual father'; and Rev. Dr. T. D. Stubblefield, who challenges me in scholarship and expository preaching; and Professor Jerram Barrs who began as one of my professors at Covenant Theological Seminary but soon became my dear friend and colleague.

I am also grateful for a few other professors at Covenant Seminary. I am grateful for New Testament professors—Drs. Jimmy

Agan and Hans Bayer—whose excitement for Greek engendered in me a voracious love for Greek as well (in case you are curious, I did well in Hebrew too but I have a special affinity for Greek). Finally, there are "three sets of feet" I would to love to tarry awhile and simply listen to their wisdom. These 'feet' belong to Drs. David Calhoun, Robert Vasholz, and David C. Jones. Dr. Calhoun taught me to love history in general and church history in particular; Drs. Vasholz and Jones are now retired, but quietly and humbly these men not only instilled in me a love for research and scholarship but they taught me not to take myself too seriously. Drs. Vasholz and Jones[1] are brilliant men and hilariously funny theologians!

Lastly, I am indebted to the indomitable Mary Purnell, my work and learn student at Lindenwood University, who formatted my bibliography page.

---

1. Sadly, Dr. Jones passed on March 5, 2017; however, his influence on me will live on.

Foreword

It is an honor and delight to be asked to write this foreword for Dr. Luke Bobo's book on the calling of each Christian to be salt and light in their workplace. Luke is a beloved brother and one of my very dearest friends. I count it a privilege to know him, to have worked alongside him and to have learned from him. Luke is eminently suited to write this book for several reasons. First, because he practices what he preaches in this book, and he practices it well. I can say this from firsthand experience because Luke and I worked together for about a decade.

Luke was the Director of the Francis Schaeffer Institute at Covenant Theological Seminary where I am a professor and the resident scholar at the Institute. I do not recall having a single question, doubt, hesitation or difficulty about Luke's abilities, about his skills at his job, about the way he treated me, his colleague, or the way he treated those who were working under his direction and who were answerable to his authority: secretaries, assistants, student interns, or the manner in which he responded to those over him in the Seminary's administration. Every day we worked together it was a joy to labor alongside each other. Ten years is a long time to spend hours every day working with a man and I would do it again gladly if the two of us ever had the opportunity. We traveled together, shared rooms on those travels, ate together, laughed together, wept together. Those years of working together, learning from each other, serving each other and growing closer with Luke are one of the most treasured memories of my more than fifty years of being in jobs of one kind or another.

So, Luke's first and most important qualification for writing about being salt and light in the workplace is this: it is my confident testimony that Luke was salt and light in our workplace for all those years, every moment of every day.

Second, Luke is an excellent student of God's Word, an absolutely necessary requirement for someone to write a book encouraging the Lord's people to serve him in their daily lives. I first met Luke when he attended an evening class I was teaching. At that time he was an engineer at Boeing and had begun to take classes in the evenings at Covenant Seminary. Luke's was one of the most eager faces in that class, one of the brightest students and one of the most humble and ready to have his mind, heart and life shaped by what he was hearing from God's Word. He was like the Bereans (about whom he writes in this book), that they were of 'more noble character' because they examined the Word of God every day to see if what Paul was teaching was faithful. Luke soon became a full-time seminary student and I grew to know him better and to value his intellectual gifts even more highly.

Luke's third qualification to write this book is that he is an excellent teacher. By the time he graduated I was eager to have him stay and to work with me in the Schaeffer Institute at the Seminary. I have described the privilege of those labors together in the paragraphs above. In that setting he had more and more opportunities to teach and we eventually ended up team-teaching classes at Covenant and teaching together when we traveled both here in the United States and overseas. Every time I have heard Luke teach I have learned from God's Word and have grown in my understanding and, I trust, in my discipleship. He is a faithful, clear, imaginative and powerful communicator of Christian truth. I wish we were still teaching together and it is a daily sorrow to me that no longer labor side by side.

That faithful, clear, imaginative and powerful communication has now found its way to the printed page in this, Luke's first book. I commend his exposition of the Christian's calling to serve God in the workplace with joy, knowing this book will be a blessing to you and will help any reader to serve the Lord more faithfully. Sit down, open your heart and mind, be ready to learn and be eager to be changed. God's passion is that you be transformed from one degree of glory to another into the likeness of his Son. This book will be an instrument in the Lord's hands to help shape you into that likeness, and to aid you as you seek to walk in the ways the Lord desires for you in your daily life.

Jerram Barrs
Professor of Christianity and Contemporary Culture
Resident Scholar of the Francis Schaeffer Institute

Introduction

Before the official introduction, I need to introduce myself. Credentials in corporate America grant people the right to be heard or, in this case, to be read. I have been working since I was 14 years of age, so I have been employed over 40 years in formal and informal workplace settings. At the age of 14, my entrepreneurial cousin and I pushed our less-than-pristine lawn mower and carried our gascan house-to-house cutting neighborhood lawns. After college, I worked in corporate America more than fifteen years including engineering internships at Allied-Signal (formerly associated with Honeywell) and Burns and McDonnell, both in Kansas City, Missouri. I worked also full-time in engineering at Allied-Signal and McDonnell Douglas Aerospace in St. Louis (now Boeing). I also worked nine years as the Director of the Francis Schaeffer Institute which is located on the campus of Covenant Theological Seminary in St. Louis. While the cultures of corporate America and the nonprofit world are quite different, there is still one common denominator: both require working and serving with broken people. Both workplace contexts, provide ample opportunities to grow in Christlikeness. In my 40 years working in formal and informal workplace settings, I have been privileged to travel extensively in the United States and abroad. I hope these credentials will convince you to keep reading.

Why another book on being "salt and light" in the workplace? Honestly, I think "in the workplace" adds a certain specificity that is often overlooked in most discussions on being salt and light.

And to be quite frank, I am disturbed and bothered by David F. Wells' assessment of the impact and influence of evangelicalism in America. He laments in *No Place for Truth or Whatever Happened to Evangelical Theology*,

> The vast growth in evangelically minded people in the 1960s, 1970s, and 1980s should by now have revolutionized American culture. With a third of American adults now claiming to have experienced spiritual rebirth, a powerful countercurrent of morality growing out of a powerful and alternative worldview should have been unleashed in factories, offices, and board rooms, in the media, universities, [laboratories], and professions, from one end of the country to the other. The results should by now be unmistakable. Secular values should be reeling, and those who are their proponents should be very troubled. But as it turns out, all of this swelling of the evangelical ranks has passed unnoticed in the culture. It has simply been absorbed and tamed. Aside from Jerry Falwell's aborted attempt from the political Right in the 1980s to roll back the earlier victories scored by the Left, especially during the 1960s, the presence of evangelicals in American culture has barely caused a ripple.[1]

Wells pinpoints a specific locale where Christians should be unleashing "a powerful countercurrent of morality"—in the workplace. Think about it; work is the most logical and likely place where Christians should be making the greatest impact. Consider the percentage of time a person spends at work—a minimum of 33% to 41% of their waking hours.[2] A former colleague at Lindenwood University (St. Charles, MO) has noted that many people will spend 90,000 hours of their lives working.

Sadly, I think Wells is correct when he concludes that " . . . the presence of evangelicals in American culture has barely caused a

1. *Wells, No Place For Truth or Whatever Happened to Evangelical Theology*, 293.

2. There are 24 hours in a day or 120 hours per 5-day workweek. So, if a person works 40 to 50 hours per week this means that 33% (40 divided by 120) to 41% (50 divided by 120) of their time is spent in the workplace.

ripple [in the workplace]." Maybe this is what a Covenant Theological Seminary professor meant when he told his class, "we are partly to blame for the state of our country (and our workplaces) because of our refusal and/or inability to be salt and light." Consider the collapse of such companies as Enron and Worldcom and, even further back, the E.F. Hutton Group. When I think about these three companies I am simply tongue-tied and find it unbelievable that they no longer exist. I have often thought there must have been Christians (*at least one*) in these companies who saw the proverbial writing on the wall. And my only logical explanation for why these collapses[3] were not averted is because Christians were not being salt and light or did not create any "waves" in these precarious contexts. So, this book is my humble attempt to encourage Christian professionals to be salt and light in the workplace and radically reverse Wells' assessment. My prayer is that this little work will in some way spark a revival among Christian workers.

ROADMAP: LAYOUT FOR BOOK

In June 2007, I was privileged to lecture in Goiânia, Brazil about the importance of contextualizing the gospel. I gave this talk five times in five different contexts. The audiences included elementary school teachers, seminarians at a Baptist seminary, seminarians at Presbyterian seminary, full-time pastors who also taught theology classes at a Bible college, and seminar participants. To contextualize the gospel simply means to "package" or "clothe" the gospel message in a way that is accessible to the audience.

How does this idea of contextualization relate to this book? When I worked in corporate America—a context—my superiors would often imply something similar to the favorite phrase of *Dragnet's* Sergeant Joe Friday: "Just the facts, ma'am." In other words, we were encouraged to say what we wanted our audience to know early in the presentation or report and leave the details for

3. Think about the untold damage in the wake of these collapses. Employees lost their jobs; top executives were fined, and some went to jail. Some even took their lives.

them to read at their leisure. So, in Part 1 (The Facts), Chapter 1 discusses vocations, and Chapter 2 moves immediately to how to be salt and light in the workplace. In Part 2, I provide the details. Chapters 3 through 6 discuss doctrines of creation, the fall of man, redemption, and restoration, respectively. These doctrines actually provide the *why* for being salt and light in the workplace.

My aim in writing and teaching is guided by two principles. The first principle is to write (or teach) to express rather than impress. I have tried to simplify hard concepts not for the purposes of "dumbing down" this material, but for the sole purpose of effectively communicating. In fact, the highest compliment after preaching came from a 13-year-old teenager who told me (via her mother) that she understood what I said. The second principle is simply to be creative and not boring. And let's face it; topics like history and theology can be quite technical and boring.

My experience as a practical theologian and an educator has convinced me of the value of teaching as a dialogue between student and teacher. I have included some questions at the end of each chapter to hone your critical thinking skills—please take the time to think through your answers as you read.

PART 1

"The Facts"

1

A Triad of Vocations

All the world's a stage,
And all the men and women merely players;
They have their exits and their entrances,
And one man in his time plays many parts,
His acts being seven ages.

—SHAKESPEARE, *AS YOU LIKE IT*, ACT 2, SCENE 7

The casting call had been broadcast in the land. "Let me see what you got." These words were uttered by my son Caleb as he, then 10 years old, played the role of a director in our church Christmas play. He and his assistants were holding auditions so that they might cast the right person in the right role. The casting director (my son) wanted to be intentional and purposeful because he had a specific goal in mind for the play. Directors, even if only playing the role of a director, must be very thoughtful about casting or placing persons in roles. A director pictures the scene in his mind and thoughtfully asks, "Will this person fit the role well?" "Will this person bring this character to life?" A director must carefully discern through auditions who should be selected for major and minor roles.

God is the director of a major drama. And God strategically, thoughtfully, and providentially[1] casts men and women in roles as He thinks about His specific goals for redemptive history. God knows where history is headed, and He appoints men and women in roles to achieve His purposes. Every Christian is called or appointed to a role. Every person has a divinely designed position. These divinely appointed or assigned roles are how I define the term vocation. God has called or appointed every Christian to three vocations or assignments: a "walking" vocation, a relational vocation, and a specific work vocation.

This triad of vocations all share these common features:

1. God has equipped you to carry out this vocation.

2. True vocations are difficult to vacate.[2]

3. All vocations are meant to be nurtured and honed.

4. All three vocations have been entrusted to us by God. We are in charge of or stewards of each vocation. This means, of course, we will give an account of our stewardship.

WALKING VOCATION

We are summoned to a "walking" vocation. In the Old Testament, "walk" often meant not literally walking on two feet, but rather referred to one's behavior. God promises Solomon that if he walks before Him as David, his father walked, then God will establish his throne forever (2 Chronicles 7:17). A bad "walking" example is King Abijam who reigned over Judah and "committed [or walked

1. Providential simply means nothing happens to us by accident; rather God orchestrates the events in our lives.

2. This probably explains in part why Michael Jordan retired three times from basketball; he was called to play basketball, and therefore found it difficult to stop.

in] all the sins his father had done before him; his heart was not fully devoted to the Lord his God, as the heart of David his forefather had been" (1 Kings 15:3).

We find the same usage of the word "walk" in the New Testament. Ephesians 4:1–2 provides a clear and compelling illustration. In the King James Version, we find these words,

> I therefore, the prisoner of the Lord, beseech you that ye *walk* worthy of the *vocation* wherewith ye are *called*, with all lowliness and meekness, with longsuffering, forbearing one another in love . . .

This passage makes it clear that we have been called to a vocation that involves "walking." In both biblical testaments, "walking" in both biblical testaments is a way of describing how we live. The Apostle Paul prescribes that we should walk or conduct ourselves in a manner worthy of the calling by which we have been called. We are to walk in a manner that corresponds to our new affiliation as Christians. In other words, what we confess with our lips should cohere with our lifestyle. Lip and lifestyle should agree.[3]

This is our common or universal vocation—walk in a manner worthy or in concert with our calling as Christians. Cornelius Plantinga explains this when he writes, "A Christian's *main vocation* is to become a prime citizen of the kingdom of God—and this is true of *every* Christian, of artists and engineers as well as ministers and evangelists (italics mine)."[4] And here's some good news: as we carry out our "walking vocation," we have a permanent walking companion. It is true that God is totally other from us, but He is also comes near to walk with us. God is truly Immanuel — God with us!

RELATIONAL VOCATION

We imitate God in a myriad of ways. God is moral; we are moral. God is rational; we are rational. God works; we are called to work

---

3. Green, *Evangelism in the Early Church*, 215.
4. Plantinga, *Engaging God's World*, 108.

with our heads, hands, and hearts. God is relational (just think of the perfect community of the Godhead); we are relational. We were made for relationships which include parent/child, contractor/client, friend, and sibling relationships. This is what it means that God has called every Christian to a relational vocation.

For some, the relational vocation means entering the holy estate of matrimony, while for others it does not. Surprise—God did not call every person to get married! Yet our American culture often assumes everyone is called to be married. Every American is expected to follow an unwritten script without deviation. And from birth we are taught to rigidly and religiously follow this script. Here's the script:

- Attend and graduate from college;
- Land a job with a fat paycheck;
- Get married;
- Buy a house with a white picket fence in the suburbs;
- Have two and ½ kids;
- Acquire a dog named Spot;
- Purchase a SUV; and
- Live happily ever after.

I once heard a very popular American TV minister encourage adherence to this script using Habakkuk 2:2b, "Write the vision." Using this verse as a launching pad, he said, "Make it a goal to be married in 10 years." I hope this TV minister reads my book, because this is ludicrous. Sadly, this minister's Christianity has become *Americanized*. I praise God for this country—for its opportunities and religious freedoms—but there is a huge difference in being an Americanized Christian and a Christian living in America. This is what I mean:

The *Americanized* Christian:

- Follows the script uncritically, no questions asked.
- Elevates the script to the status of authoritative doctrine.

- Pledges his allegiance religiously and unflinchingly to a political party.

The Christian living in America:

- Lives under the lordship of Christ, which means he or she will carefully weigh the opinions of the land versus God's opinion. For instance, the Christian living in America, will ask, "God, are you calling me to the holy estate of matrimony? Or are you calling me to the holy estate of singleness?"

- Critically evaluates political party affiliation from a Christian worldview. For instance, I remember telling a group of students at McKendree College (now McKendree University in Lebanon, Illinois) before the 2004 presidential election, "It would irresponsible for you to vote based on how your family has historically voted." Many students had that deer-in-the-headlights stunned look after I made that statement.

RESPONSE TO SCRIPT

I have many questions for the TV minister who endorsed the American script. Do we really have that much control of our destiny? What happens if you don't follow this script? What if marriage or college isn't for you? During a retreat, I remember telling some engineering majors who were attending the University of Cape Town, South Africa that some of them were not called to the rigors of academia. You would have thought I had uttered an expletive because many of their mouths dropped! Prior to this talk, I heard from many students who were taking medication to cope with the stress of academia—this was a clear indication my words were on the mark for some of these students.[5] I know several people who have done well by their families and didn't go to college. My late grandfather, Henry Bobo, was a star athlete in high school and had a chance to go to college, but was called to serve in World War II.

5. Another reason for the high stress and anxiety was many of these kids were first-generation college students and their families placed great hope in them. That pressure certainly added to their stress.

After serving in the Navy, he mastered the trade of brick masonry. Two of his three kids attended and graduated from college, and his firstborn son went to a two-year community college. My grandfather did not own a credit card. His wife, my late grandmother, Willa Mae Bobo, was a content, proud housewife and wanted for nothing. My family is not unique in this regard. Other families can parade members who did well without going to college—because college is not meant for everyone and that's okay!

Similarly, not every married couple is called to be parents. God is the Lord of the womb; which means that He opens and closes the womb. We can call several witnesses to the stand, namely, Sarah, Hannah, Elizabeth, and Rachel. Each one would say unequivocally, "Yes, the Lord is indeed Lord of the womb." The bottom line is that we cannot presume upon His gracious sovereign will for our lives.

Not every person is called to wed. God has called some of us to singleness. Just consider the Apostle Paul in 1 Corinthians 7:8 and the late Mother Theresa. When I counsel engaged couples I ask them, "How do you know you have been called to marry?" As Christians, we need to be aware that our Christianity is often an Americanized version of Christianity. Instead of walking lock, stock, and barrel in line with the American script, we must seek God's direction and wisdom in all areas of life, for He promises to give it generously (James 1:5).

SPECIFIC VOCATIONS

The third type of vocation we are called to is our specific God-given work assignments. Every Christian has specific and divinely ordained work in the marketplace. I am using marketplace to mean that public place God has called you to—home, workplace, military, etc. Adam and Eve's vocation was to care for the garden. Some Christians are called to vocations in the church; some are called to vocations in secular companies. Some are called to be ministers; some are called to be lawyers. Some are called to be missionaries; some are called to be nurses. Some are called to be athletes; some are called to be seminary professors. Some are called to be CEOs; some are called to be housewives or musicians or artists. Some are called to be golfers; some are called to be land keepers. Some are called to be politicians; some are called to be priests or nuns. Some are called to be plumbers, electricians, painters, or carpenters, and God has called some to work in the service industry as maids, housekeepers, janitors, etc. Whatever our specific calling, God has uniquely and divinely equipped each of us to perform this work assignment to His glory (Colossians 3:23-25).

NO HIERARCHY OF VOCATIONS

The late Dr. Francis Schaeffer wrote a book entitled *No Little People* based on the thesis that there are no little places and no little people. Taking some liberties to amend this thesis slightly, I would say, there are no little places, no little people, and *no little vocations*. In other words, I detect no pecking order or hierarchy of vocations in Scripture. All vocations that seek the common good of all have inherent dignity and worth. By common good, I mean those vocations that aid and abet flourishing for all human beings.

I remember a very prominent pastor saying from the pulpit, "I have the most important job in the world." That attitude is elitist and arrogant, and it devalues the work of others. In fact, I believe the Christians with the greatest challenges are those who must rub elbows with unbelievers on a day-to-day basis in the workplace. Isn't it interesting that God called workers prior to deploying them into another calling or vocation? God called former shepherds David and Amos to lead and serve as spokesmen to His people. God called fishermen Peter, James, and John as apostles. God called Luke, a physician, to be Paul's traveling companion and the author of the two-volume set, Luke-Acts.

Part 1: "The Facts"

AN AGE OLD DICHOTOMY: LET'S BURY IT!

Imagine one monk saying to another monk, "This weekend, let's do something secular." The cartoon in Figure 1 tickles our funny bone to be sure; however, it also teaches us at least two lessons. First, the cartoon suggests that we can live a compartmentalized life—a secular life and a sacred life. This is not true for the Christian. A former seminary professor puts it this way, "For the Christian, there is no such thing as a secular moment." Second, the monastery is normally considered a place where great sacrifice has been offered and truly sacred work occurs. This notion has encouraged that old dichotomy of the spiritual versus the secular. This dichotomy, which still has a powerful effect, can encourage us to regard spiritual vocations as more valuable than secular vocations.

Figure 1: From the *Wall Street Journal,* permission Cartoon Features Syndicate, March 17, 2017.

14

Some Christians live by this sacred vs. secular dichotomy. Consider these few examples: A Christian elementary teacher said, "I don't have time to do something for the Lord because of my day job." By making this statement she was declaring that her day job as an elementary school teacher is secular and therefore, less important than spiritual work such as preparing a Sunday School lesson or being a foreign missionary. Or well-meaning Christians may say, "Only what you do for Christ will last." Typically, this comment means that spiritual work such as being a pastor, foreign missionary, or Sunday School worker is far more important than working inside or outside the home. Or consider this comment from a prominent pastor in the Midwest, addressing his congregation: "Christians should not work for places like Anheuser Busch."[6] In his defense, this pastor had good intentions as he is aware of how alcohol has wreaked havoc on many communities and our society. However, while his intentions are noble, there are huge problems with his mandate.

First, doesn't a place like Anheuser Busch need Christians who are salt and light? Second, if alcohol is a culprit that negatively affects human lives, why not say that Christians should not work for companies like Boeing Aerospace[7] (my former employer) because they manufacture jets or airborne weapons that not only annihilate buildings and bridges but also kill people? Third, what do we make of Christians living in other cultures that drink alcohol unabashedly (Italians love their wine; Germans love their beer)? Who is the final arbitrator of such matters? Fourth, what criteria does we use to decide if a Christian should work for this company or that company, and can we apply this criterion consistently? And what about the Christian who owns and operates a bar? Should we shun or condemn this person? I know a fine Christian man who owns and operates a bar-restaurant and does so with great wisdom and care.

6. Anheuser Busch (now InBev), which is headquartered in St. Louis, MO, is one of the leading manufacturers of beer and beer products.

7. When I was an engineer at Boeing, the company was still McDonnell Douglas Aerospace.

Both the pastor and the elementary teacher are essentially asserting that only full-time vocational ministry tasks are considered significant in God's economy and worthy of our time and attention. Sadly, both are examples of secular-versus-spiritual thinking that is profoundly unbiblical. However, this pastor and elementary school teacher are not alone; many Christians fail to see how their 9-to-5 jobs can actually advance God's kingdom or His rule. Both this pastor and elementary school teacher fail to see how 9-to-5 work can actually push back the darkness. Perhaps, Gene Veith can help this pastor, elementary teacher and us to see differently. He writes, "God calls people to different kinds of labor as part of His governance of the world. God Himself is operative in human labor."[8] God is at work through your work and in your workplace.

In God's opinion, all vocations are deemed worthy and important. Just consider these truths about the Bible:

First, if jobs or occupations we classify as secular were not important to God, why would He direct His writers to include them in the Bible? Consider this small sampling:

- In 1 Kings 4:1–6, we find Solomon was king and his staff included Elihoreph and Ahijah as secretaries, Jehoshaphat as a recorder, Ahishar in charge of the palace, and Adorniram in charge of the forced labor.

- In Amos 1:1, we find that Amos was a shepherd.

- In Acts 9:43, we find Peter stayed with Simon, a tanner. In Titus 3:13, we find Zenas the lawyer.

- In Colossians 4:14, we find Luke the beloved physician.

- In Romans 16:23, we find Erastus, the city treasurer.

Second, not once are we told that the Apostle Paul, minister to the Gentiles, jettisoned his blue-collar trade as a tentmaker. In fact, we are told in Philippians that he employed his skills as a tentmaker so that he would not be a burden on the Christians at Philippi. We might say Paul was bi-vocational.

8. Gene Veith, *God at Work: Your Christian Vocation in All of Life*, 65.

And we can assume that Jesus was a carpenter for many years. Jesus, our Savior, handled a hammer and nails. Imagine that! Jesus' disciples, who were fishermen before Christ summoned them, resumed their professions after Jesus died and ascended to heaven. The layperson's vocation is just as valuable as the pastor's vocation; the home as a workplace is just as important as the car mechanic's garage. Because human workers are made in God's image and because all human beings have value and worth, we make these vocations and workplaces significant. In other words, instead of deriving meaning *from* our work; we bring meaning *to* our work and our workplaces.

REDEEMING AN UNCOMMON PRACTICE

The church has an excellent opportunity to redeem an uncommon practice. What is this uncommon practice? We seem to have a default position. We celebrate members of our churches and in our society who hold white-collar jobs—lawyers, politicians, educators, engineers, pilots, and businessmen and women. So, here's a novel concept; let's celebrate *all* workers. Make this uncommon practice a common practice. Let those who are brothers and sisters in Christ advocate celebrating members of our churches who have blue-collar jobs as well as those with white-collar jobs. Let's celebrate and affirm the factory line worker; our mailman/woman; the janitor; the painter; the plumber; and the guy or lady who collects our trash from the curb during the week.

DISCOVERING YOUR SPECIFIC WORK ASSIGNMENT

Every Christian has divinely appointed work assignments. Some people are aware early in life of their specific work assignment. For example, Tiger Woods at the age of three was swinging a golf club. It was inevitable that he would play golf. A police officer who serves in Lake St. Louis City, MO, once told me that when he was only five years old he told his mom that he wanted to be a police officer. My friend Jerram Barrs tells the story of his nephew. His first words were mommy and daddy; the next word out of his mouth was "ca-ca" (for car). Jerram's nephew spent many years as a car mechanic. And he was quite good at it.

For most of us, finding our work vocation is a journey. God may take you on intentional or providential detours or to places of preparation prior to landing you in a specific vocation. My detour started in engineering for fifteen-year stint to to being an administrative director for nine years to finally to Lindenwood University as an associate professor of Christian Ministry Studies.

Unfortunately, if the authors of *Finding a Job You Can Love* are right, 50 to 80 percent of people in the workforce are in the wrong jobs or vocations.[9] Here are some practical questions to ask yourself as you search for your divinely appointed work assignment:

- What do you daydream about?

- Who is doing what you want to do?

- What do you have a passion for? Or said another way, what would get you out of bed in the morning?

- If money and bills were of no concern, what would you do?

- When do you feel God's delight? I sense God's delight when I am teaching. Without appearing proud, I not only enjoy teaching but it is not difficult. Teaching comes naturally to me.

- What is it that you do that causes people to say, "Wow, you were great, you do that so effortlessly"?

When I was writing this book, my beautiful daughter Briana was a freshman at a major university. She switched from majoring in international marketing to political science and finally to journalism (with a minor in Spanish). Switching majors is okay as many of us switched several times before deciding on a major. However, I firmly believe that my daughter has been called to be a writer and her major in journalism was indeed the right choice. When my wife

9. Mattson and Miller, *Finding a Job You Can Love*, 123.

and I read some of her work, we are just blown away. My daughter wrote so well in middle school that her science teacher thought she had plagiarized someone else's work. With my daughter's permission, I have included a poem she penned in "literally 35 minutes" (her words) entitled "Winged Sleeper." It is a poem about my dearly beloved grandmother, Willa Mae Bobo, on the night she died.

Winged Sleeper

In a hospital room,
on a cold afternoon,
  she died,
and in doing so
gained a second life
A permanent sleep
  ironic,
deep sleep meaning already deceased
Is not sleep supposed to calm, revive and refresh?
instead as she lay, her spirit escaped
the body remained
that sweet smile, endearing demeanor
coyly retreated
  gone now forever,
Except for in memories,
pictures and mental diaries
  amongst the angels, the greatest honor
frolicking with God's beloved, most faithful
In a hospital room,
on a cold afternoon,
  she died,
  her wings already in place
no longer here
in transition to destination improved
  she's finally free to fly.

Recall that one of the diagnostic questions I proposed for identifying your divinely appointed work assignment is allowing others to give you a verbal and objective assessment. What work are you engaged in where people say, "Wow, you were great; you do that so effortlessly"? For example, I sent this poem to Dr. Michael Castro, my former colleague at Lindenwood University, to get his assessment before I disclosed my daughter as the poet so as to not influence Castro's assessment. He said, "The poem is heartfelt [and] well written [and] applies free verse [and] line breaks in knowing ways, so it's written in a modern manner." If you do a Google search on Michael Castro, you will discover that he is well known in the literary world—he knows what he's talking about!

SOME COSTS

I need to confess something to you: pursuing your specific or divinely appointed work assignment will take courage, and it will cost you. It may cost you your title, prestige, standard of living, and the size of your paycheck. I remember a woman I'll call Vicki from when I was Minister of Christian Education at a local church in St. Louis. I observed Vicki at church and noticed her obvious teaching gifts. At the time, she worked in the computer or information technology (IT) field. I encouraged her to teach a Sunday school class for elementary-school-age kids. She started teaching young people and loved it so much she quit her IT job and pursued what she discovered to be her divinely appointed work to be an elementary school teacher. This career switch cost her a handsome salary as an IT professional but she couldn't be more happy and content. Vicki sent this message to me via e-mail:

> What's up Rev!
> Yes, I am moving back to Arkansas in June. It's time to get back and enjoy the family. I'm going to miss my Christian family in St. Louis.
> Yep, I'm a teacher also. I teach 6th and 7th grade math for St. Louis City Public Schools. Thanks to my big bro (Luke), who called me to teach Sunday school (hint,

hint), I decided to pursue my lifelong dream of teaching professionally. I love it!! Even my bad days as a teacher are better than my good days as a computer programmer. I know in my heart that God has chosen me to be in this profession.

Think about it. When you do what you were divinely designed to do, the result must be contentment and exhilaration because you are *working as designed*. It makes sense that if Christians worked in fields where they were divinely designed to serve, there would be less stress, less drudgery, less hypertension, and less debt to name a few. And you will gain contentment and joy—which are priceless!

DISCUSSION QUESTIONS

1. How is your "walking" vocation? Is it healthy?

2. Have you discovered what you have been divinely designed to do? If so, are you doing it? Why or why not?

3. Have you bought into the idea that one's script is to go to college, get married, have children, etc.? Why or why not?

4. Do you understand what is meant by the spiritual/secular divide? How will you seek to eradicate this mistaken idea?

2

Salt and Light in the Workforce: Another Vocation

"You are the salt of the earth and
You are the light of the world."

—JESUS CHRIST

This is the chapter where the rubber meets the road. In other words, this chapter will answer the *how* of being salt and light in the workplace. Imagine you are at a seminar on how to be salt and light in the workplace. That means of course we need a PowerPoint presentation. My first slide provides the agenda or what I plan to cover in this chapter:

- Clear pattern in Scripture

- What salt and light *is not*

- Exposition of Matthew 5:13–16

- What salt and light *is*

- How to break money's grip on us
- Reasons we don't use our influence
- Two semi-trailer trucks (or two formidable forces that make being salt and light difficult)
- Implications of this historical moment
- Christians with no influence
- Apologetics in the workplace
- Some "final words" and a prayer

CLEAR PATTERN IN SCRIPTURE

Discerning readers of Scripture will see a clear and persistent pattern. What is that pattern? God graciously and providentially acts on our behalf and commands that we respond in gratitude. God initiates a relationship with us, saves us, redeems us, pursues us, and rescues us, and then He asks that we respond by giving generously, serving others, and obeying and praising Him. In Exodus 20:2 Moses states what God has done: "I am the Lord your God, who brought you out of the land of Egypt, out of the house of slavery"; now in gratitude to me for what I have done, obey these Ten Commandments (Exodus 20:3–17). You see the order? God works on our behalf; we then work for God. In Romans 1–11, Paul systematically and masterfully tells the church at Rome (and us) what God has done; in Romans 12–15 we are told how to respond. Being salt and light in the workplace is a response to what God has graciously done and continues to do for us. We will cover what God has done for us in more detail in Chapter 4: Some Marvelous Good News: Redemption!

WHAT SALT AND LIGHT IS NOT

By being salt and light in the workplace, I *do not mean*:
- Peppering your workspace with Scriptures

- Having one of those fish emblems prominently displayed on your car
- Wearing a large cross around your neck
- Prominently displaying a Bible in your work space
- Quietly playing Christian music in the background
- Using Christian tracts as bargaining chips or requiring co-workers to take a tract before you will answer their questions
- Signing your emails with scripture or Christian phrases
- Having Bible tracts prominently displayed in your work area

There's nothing inherently wrong with playing Christian music in your workspace or including a meaningful scripture in your email signature. However, these Christian symbols or practices can feel confrontational or too "in your face," especially if separated from building relationship and working in a way to represent Christ.

There is a better way. To give you a preview, consider this question: what negative or unbiblical descriptors come to mind when you think of corporate America? Here's my partial list:

Greed—think about top-paid executives who are either fired or leave voluntarily with multi-million-dollar severance packages.

Compromised Integrity—for example, fudging on or "massaging" some data or facts for political reasons, like bosses who encourage their employees to fudge the business trip expense report.

Mistreatment of Employees—I think of the character Milton in the movie *Office Space*. Without giving too much away, I recommend that you watch the film with friends and discuss how employees are treated by management and fellow employees.

"Watergates"—there are numerous cover-ups to save face or someone's backside.

Unhealthy Pressures—many employees are encouraged to work an insane amount of hours, which takes away from family time and makes them forfeit bodily rest.

Slander and Grumbling—in so much of our culture, it is normal to participate in raking the boss' name over the coals or griping about coworkers.

Being salt and light in the workplace means doing and being 180 degrees opposite of the negative descriptors enumerated above. To understand what it looks like to be salt and light in the workplace, let's look at where this imagery comes from in the Bible.

EXPOSITION OF MATTHEW 5:13-16

This language of "salt" and "light" comes from Matthew 5:13-16, which is part of Jesus' Sermon on the Mount. This famous sermon was addressed to His disciples, while a great many people listened in. In the sermon, Jesus provides both a list of personal kingdom ethics for the Christian for living in a broken world and an ethical system for corporate living in the body of Christ.

Jesus tells His disciples that "*you are*[1] the salt of the earth and *you are* the light of the world." What does statements mean for the identity of the Christian worker?

The literal translation of verses 13 and 14 is: "*you, you are* the salt of the earth" and "*you, you are* the light of the world." Matthew's repetition of the word *you* is meant to convey emphasis. An eye-witness reporter who heard the sermon being preached, Matthew is doing his best to capture both what and how Jesus is communicating this message. Matthew has captured Jesus being emphatic (the "*you, you are . . .*" tell us this). Jesus is not fumbling over or mincing His words; He is being very demonstrative in saying "Hey, brothers and sisters—you are the salt of the earth and you are the light of the world at all times"!

---

1. A grammatical analysis of the verb suggests this is *always* true—in every place and at all times.

Jesus, the master teacher, specialized in contextualizing His teaching. Jesus uses two common elements or staples of daily life in Jerusalem as teaching metaphors: salt and light. That means we must ask what the purpose of salt and light are and how they apply to working in our broken workplaces.

Salt is used to slow or limit decay. Turner elaborates, "The salt is an image of a preservative. In the absence of refrigeration, it was what his [Jesus'] audience put on their fish and meat. It didn't bring life to the flesh, but it *slowed down the process of decay* (italics mine)."[2] A Jamaican colleague of mine often tells the story of his dad taking him fishing when he was a little boy. When they caught a fish, his daddy would lay a bed of salt and then place the fish on top. Before laying more fish on top, his dad added another layer of salt. His daddy sandwiched the fish between layers of salt to slow down its decay.

Light is used to displace darkness. Take any light into a dark space, and it will displace or overcome the darkness. Again, Turner illuminates the importance of this metaphor, noting that "the light is an image of guidance and revelation. With a candle or lamp you could know where you were and could explore without being hampered."[3]

WHAT SALT AND LIGHT IS

Being salt and light in the workplace does mean that we work to expose corruption and give guidance to others; and when we do, we will actually slow down the process of sin's decaying impact in the workplace and cause more than ripples. In other words, we can work in such a way to put positive pressure on our peers.

2. Turner, *Imagine: A Vision for Christians in the Arts*, 69.

3. Turner, 69–70.

Peer Pressure

As disciples (like Jesus' disciples), we " . . . constitute the salt and light without which the earth cannot survive and remains in darkness."[4] In other words, your workplace cannot survive without your salty and light-filled life. Remember how I began with the collapse of Enron, Worldcom, and E.F. Hutton?

Moreover, you must work in such a way that you are not only visible but that you actually and positively influence your fellow peers. Jerry Bridges reminds us that Christians should be " . . . exemplary in every aspect of life."[5] This certainly includes being exemplary employees. When we are exemplars, we influence the thinking and behavior of our coworkers. Salty and light-filled workers influence their peers; they push back the effects of sin and expose darkness (corruption).

LIVING AS SALT AND LIGHT AS AN EMPLOYEE

What does it look like to live this out? Here are some practical ways to be salt and light if you work for someone in any workplace.

Meditate on God's Word

We cannot begin to talk about how to be salt and light in the workforce without first talking about our duty to be diligent students of God's word. In Psalm 1, which is categorized as a wisdom psalm, we are reminded to meditate upon God's word day and night. Such meditation is not of the variety associated with Near Eastern religions. In God's economy, to meditate means to think about, ponder, or contemplate His thoughts. The image of meditating on God's word is like that of two tennis players hitting a ball back and forth. We are to volley God's word back and forth in our minds. This is necessary so that we can think God's thoughts, facilitate the

---

4. Hagner, Word Biblical Commentary on Matthew, 102.

5. Bridges, *Disciplines of Grace*, 87.

process of renewing our minds, and to undo the impact of secularism and postmodernism on our thoughts and behaviors. We'll discuss postmodernism and secularism more a bit later.

Discerning Sound Christian Doctrine

The unfortunate reality today is that sound Christian doctrine is in danger. Doctrine is becoming an endangered species. There are many claims to orthodoxy on parade, but they are often counterfeits. Additionally, we live in a culture that has no shortage of "authoritative" voices. Remember the wrist bands with the initials WWJD (what would Jesus Do)? Now we must add wristbands with WWOS (what would Oprah say?) and WWDPS (what would Dr. Phil say?). And add to these authoritative options a bumper sticker I saw that asked WWBD (what would Buddha do?).

Crist offers a very telling insight, noting that we live " . . . in a culture where Deepak Chopra, Oprah Winfrey and Larry Dossey are more authoritative voices than Moses, Jesus, or even Mohammed . . ."[6] Therefore, commit yourself to diligent and dutiful study of God's word and to learning in a Christian community where the teaching of sound doctrine is preeminent. As we learn in private and in community we can mutually edify and challenge each other because no Christian's worldview is immune from the corrosive creep of bad doctrine and ideas antithetical to Christianity. Preachers must challenge their congregations to adhere to the Berean principle. The Scripture says " . . . they [Berean Jews] received the word with all eagerness, examining[7] the Scriptures daily to see if these things were so (Acts 17:11)." Surely, these Bereans had heard the reports about the Apostle Paul and had probably seen his impressive curriculum vitae:[8]

- a pure-blooded Jew

6. Crist, *Learning the Language of Babylon: Changing the World by Engaging the Culture*, 151.

7. The word translated as "examine" means that they engaged in careful study of the Scriptures.

8. For some of Paul's credentials see Philippians 3:1–11.

- studied at the feet of the prominent teacher Gamaliel
- as to the law blameless
- a Pharisee of the Pharisees
- one who excelled beyond his contemporaries

Yet, *they examined what Paul said through the filter of Scripture daily.* For the Bereans it was not about a mere emotional response; they did not check their minds at the synagogue door. Rather they engaged their minds. An analysis of the word "examine" suggests they practiced this discipline continuously. While giving his testimony, a professor at the University of Cape Town explained that "believing Christianity is not intellectual suicide." As Christians, we must examine the Scriptures daily and not take a communicator of God's word at face value. Otherwise, we would be committing intellectual suicide. When I preach, I frequently encourage congregations to keep their Bibles open to keep me honest! Diligent study of good doctrine will assure us that we are actually behaving as salty and light-filled Christians in the workplace.

Prayer

Pray earnestly for men and women at all levels of management. It is not easy managing broken people. If you have children, consider how difficult it is to manage them! Pray for those brothers and sisters in Christ who are in management. Just imagine the relentless tug-of-war they are in engaged in on a daily basis between toeing the party line or going against the stream. Professionally speaking, these men and women are your superiors, but you have a familial relationship with them too. If they believe in Christ, these men and women are chiefly your brothers and sisters in Christ. Even if they are not, they are still made in the image of God, and God calls us to pray for one another. Pray for those coworkers or supervisors that mistreat or slander you. And pray for the salvation of your coworkers and supervisors.

One of the chief idols that competes for our allegiance is the idol of personal freedom. Serving this idol is not a benign affair; it is not inconsequential. Serving this idol will lead to isolation and loneliness, to a disconnection from people. God has called us to community for mutual encouragement. So, I strongly encourage you to pray that God will provide you an accountability partner. Because of this demanding idol—the idol of personal freedom— the need is all the more urgent to petition God for someone who can encourage and challenge you to walk in holiness without compromise.

Heed Jesus' words: "Be Wise as a Serpent and Gentle (or Innocent) as a Dove"[9]

It is startling to see the words serpent and dove in the same sentence, but that contrast is what Jesus is showing in this passage. Contextually, Jesus is warning His disciples about the persecution that missionary disciples will face and must endure. So He urges them to be wise as a serpent—the symbol of shrewdness and intellectual cunning (see Genesis 3:1; Psalm 58:4-5) and gentle as a dove—the symbol of simple innocence (see Hosea 7:11).[10] Our workplaces are a mission field so these words indeed apply to us. For example, Christian professionals must be wise and discerning in interpreting hidden messages. Diversity training provides a good case study in this regard. I favor cultural diversity; I believe that God delights in cultural diversity. Diversity training is especially vital as our global neighbors are now our coworkers. Our coworkers are not only Christian, but Muslim, Hindu, and Buddhists. However, diversity training is oftentimes also an appeal to tolerate or endorse sinful lifestyles. A friend of mine tells me he was asked to tolerate or endorse the lifestyle of homosexuals following diversity training in the workplace. He politely refused. If asked, Christian professionals, must unapologetically and gently give an explanation for why homosexuality is out of step with God's design. Notice, I said if asked, as we must earn the right to

9. See Matthew 10:16.

10. See *English Standard Version Study Bible*, 1840.

be heard and asked. We earn the right to be heard by living out our Christian faith gently and honorably, not by arguing or obnoxiously declaring our beliefs.

You may remember my mentioning a friend who owns and operates a bar-restaurant. This man is an elder in his church, and he knows the importance of being wise as a serpent and gentle as a dove. He is acutely aware of this importance since he serves alcohol. He thinks about the number of accidents caused by drunken drivers. He thinks about the many instances where an intoxicated husband abused his wife. For him, sometimes being wise and gentle means refusing to serve a customer a drink. As you can imagine, this is typically not a pleasant exchange. His employees have been charged to be wise and gentle too. He has trained his employees to spot customers that have had too much to drink. Similarly, his employees have refused to serve inebriated customers more alcohol. My friend sometimes takes being wise and gentle a step further, calling for a cab for customers that are not sober enough to drive a vehicle. And he will also pick up the tab for the cab fare. Can you imagine how shrewd and gentle he needs to be to convince a drunk customer not to drive home?

Do Not Participate in Corruption

During my travels to a foreign country, our party met a federal judge who is a Christian. Let's call him Mike. In this country, residents have come to expect that their political and judicial leaders are corrupt. Mike, on the other hand, stands upright by upholding Christian values in a corrupt legal system. He is constantly courted to take bribes, and he is often threatened by those who want him to tip the scales of justice in favor of certain people. Each time he has refused. Is there a cost? Absolutely. He and his family have to live in a gated community with guards. But the Apostle Paul told Timothy that everyone who desires to live a godly (salty and light-filled) life will be persecuted (2 Timothy 3:12). If you rub your hands together, you will feel some heat. Heat is caused by two objects being rubbed together in opposite directions (we engineers call this friction). Anytime we go against the mainstream (the status quo) by resolving to be ethical, we can expect friction and heat. It's unavoidable. And, dear reader, Scripture *promises* you will suffer some heat (see 2 Timothy 3:12 and John 16:33). So don't be surprised when you are shunned, not invited to lunch, or not invited to staff parties. However, you can take comfort in Jesus' words, "Blessed are you when others revile you and persecute you and utter all kinds of evil against you falsely on my account" (Matthew 5:11). When Christian professionals practice Christian ethics, it is so rare and so refreshingly different that your coworkers can't help but take notice. Sometimes your coworkers will be delighted and honor you; but sometimes they will take offense.

Nonconformists

At one university where I taught 20-somethings, I often gave what I call "love talks." Because I developed a good rapport with most of them, I could challenge them. One day I asked a class of students why they came to class late and/or turned in late and often sloppy assignments? After several students voiced their opinions and justifications, another student piped up and said, "Professor Bobo, it's the culture here. Christian students just conform to the culture of tardiness, absenteeism, etc." My reply was, "God calls you all to be salt and light; to live radically different from your peers; to not be conformed to the culture around you." These are not my words; they are Paul's words in Romans 12:1–2: "Do not conform to this world." By analogy, Christians are immersed in a workplace culture. The workplace culture has a language, mores, and a code of ethics (sometimes written, most times unwritten). On one hand, we should affirm the good of our company's culture; on the other hand, we must be willing to be courageous and go against the tide if a company's cultural ethics are in conflict with our Christian ethics. In other words, we must resist conforming and compromising our values.

Equality, Not Favors

If we work for Christian managers, we should not expect or demand preferential treatment as this puts these managers in an awkward position. For example, when a brother in Christ is aware that his boss is a Christian, he may ask for leniency for meeting a deadline. This is inappropriate (unless, of course, it is for a very good reason). This is like presuming upon God's grace, which is deeply disturbing to the Lord. Additionally, James, the Lord's brother, warns us in James 2:1–7 against giving some brothers and sisters special treatment. Don't force your boss to commit the sin of partiality by granting you favors just because you and your boss are both believers in Christ.

Be People of Truth

Sometimes our supervisors will not ask us to lie outright but to fudge the truth a bit. You know the routine. After reviewing your PowerPoint slides, a supervisor may tell you, "Instead of saying it that way, say it this way." We are often told the reason for such tweaking is "political." However, all of this smells, looks, and tastes like deception. We are people of truth. Do you see the rub? As Christians, we must take courage in Christ and be willing to say, "I don't feel comfortable doing that." Stand on truth. I am not naïve—this may cost you a promotion or even your job. But in his *Oration in Memory of Abraham Lincoln*, Frederick Douglass reminds us that "*truth* is proper and beautiful at all times and in all places . . ."[11] Truth is beautiful at all times and in all workplaces.

Christians who are nonconformists, who are people of truth, who do not participate in corruption, and who operate by a different work ethic in the workplace should heed Jesus' words: "Be wise as a serpent and gentle as a dove." You will surely suffer persecution from some, but you will attract others (my guarantee.) I met Tim in Baltimore when I was teaching an adult Sunday school class on being salt and light in the workplace. Tim was asked to

11. http://www.members.tripod.com/~american_almanac/dougorat.htm.

do something contrary to his integrity at a major company, but he refused and was fired as a consequence. Tim was persecuted for going against the grain.

On the other hand, consider Michael, a young man I met at Covenant Theological Seminary, who said about his life before seminary, "my ministry at the time was my workplace." It was reported that "Michael offered a listening ear and a heart of compassion as coworkers confided in him during difficult situations. Over time God used Michael to water and cultivate seeds of faith that had been planted in the hearts of several coworkers, and he had the privilege of seeing some of them drawn into relationship with the Lord."[12] Amen! Tim and Michael represent the highs and the lows of being salt and light in the workplace.

PRACTICAL WAYS TO BE SALT AND LIGHT IF YOU ARE THE BOSS

Here I have in mind two types of people: those who supervise or manage others in the workplace, and those who are self-employed.

Christian Managers

The practices and values I have been describing for Christian employees apply to Christian managers as well, but the authority that managers wield gives them additional responsibilities. Every person bears God's image. This means every person must be treated with dignity and respect. I often heard as an engineer that employees were the company's greatest resource. For the Christian manager, this means remembering that employees are human beings and not expendable resources. From the teaching and model of Jesus in Mark 10:35–45, leaders are not to be like capricious Gentile leaders who might strike a servant without warrant or

---

12. Fogas, Student Profile: *Shaping of a Shepherd*, Covenant Magazine, Spring 2008.

warning when the urge hit them. Rather, Jesus instructs us to lead by serving others, just as He did.

Sometimes employees need to be reprimanded or fired. Yet these two challenging tasks can be done while still treating employees with grace, dignity, and respect. Sometimes, firing a person is actually a wise and loving thing to do. Otherwise, we are allowing poor work skills and enabling bad behavior. Being a Christian manager is indeed a great challenge. Yet, I encourage you not to play the game if it compromises your values and integrity as a Christian.

As a Christian manager, you are also responsible for fighting and exposing injustices. A common injustice, which is also sadly common in some of our churches, is pay inequality between the genders. Women who have the same credentials as their male counterparts are often paid less. I find this repulsive, especially since we live in the 21st century! As a Christian, you are called to use your influence to balance the scales.

Christian managers should also be careful not to lord their authority over others. The teacher is required of God to be respectful of his or her students. The coach must be respectful of his or her players, not berating players or treating them as property. Christian managers are not called to give other Christian employees preferential treatment but rather to treat their employees and customers fairly and justly.

Tom knows exactly the point I am making. As the former CEO of a major securities business in St. Louis, he said his priorities were clients first, his employees second, and the company third. In other words, his focus was not on making a profit or lining his pocket; rather his focus was the Golden Rule. He believed that if you treated clients and employees like you want to be treated, then they would remain loyal. He was emphatic about this point, saying, "I didn't preach it, but I lived it out." Tom purposely kept his and other upper management personnel salaries modest. Employees shared in the profits and were given the option to participate in a stock option program. Because Tom lived out the gospel before his employees and clients, and made certain his management staff treated employees and clients with respect, his company enjoyed record growth in their industry. Tom served as CEO from the mid-1960s until his retirement in 2001. He was so well-loved and respected that he continued to get boxes of cards from employees until his death; many of these employees never met Tom in person but wanted to wish him well and express their heartfelt thanks.

Self-Employed

A Christian self-employed person must use balanced scales; in other words, they must offer their product or service with integrity. They are called to treat the customer with respect and dignity. The Christian entrepreneur is in business to make money and must of course be competitive, but not at the expense of the customer, who is a human being made in God's image. This means that the cost of goods and services must be fair and reasonable.

Our Christian worldview strongly encourages us to be thoughtful about our business practices. The Bible gives several principles for Christian business owners. For instance, in the book of Ruth, Ruth was allowed to glean barley from Boaz's field and not pay. Why? Because Ruth was poor and a foreigner in the land (in other words, she was an immigrant). In the Year of Jubilee, employers cleared every debtor of his or her debt; what would our country look like if businesses operated by Christians cleared their debtors of their debt or substantially reduced their debt? Of course, bankruptcy laws also allow for debt relief so I am not speaking in blanket terms. However, Christian business owners should engage their imaginations to find creative ways to love their neighbor as themselves—especially, relative to a neighbor's debt relief. Additionally, Christian owners are to be governed by the mandates of Scripture, not their industry's mandates. And sometimes this will make us look odd to our contemporaries, but we are called to be a peculiar people.

COMMON TEMPTATION FOR THE BOSSES, EMPLOYEES, AND SELF-EMPLOYED PERSONS

I believe the greatest temptation for the boss, employee, and self-employed person is the love of money. Scripture addresses this in 1 Timothy 6:6–10, where Paul is exposing the greed of false teachers.[13]

> 6 Now there is great gain in godliness with contentment, 7 for we brought nothing into the world. 8 But if we have food and clothing, with these we will be content. 9 But those who desire to be rich fall into temptation, into a snare, into many senseless and harmful desires that plunge people into ruin and destruction. 10 For the love of money[14] is a root of all kinds of evils. It is through this craving that some have wandered away from the faith and pierced themselves with many pangs.

1 Timothy 6:10 is quoted often, but the verses that come before it are amazingly insightful. There is great gain in godliness with contentment. When I seek to lead a godly life coupled with contentment, I have truly gained. Paul refers to contentment (for the Christian) as an attitude of mind independent of externals and dependent only on God. These folks are truly rich.

Contentment comes with having the bare necessities of life (e.g., food, clothing, etc.).[15] Of course, the bare necessities of life is a relative phrase as these necessities will look different in every society. But it's probably less than we think. The relentless pursuit of money and things brings a hefty price tag; those with this insatiable craving fall into temptation,[16] get entangled like an animal in a snare or a deadly trap, and finally plunge into an abyss

---

13. Lea and Griffin, *The New American Commentary: An Exegetical and Theological Exposition of Holy Scripture NIV Text 1,2 Timothy and Titus*, 167–171.

14. The term translated as 'love of money' is one word in the Greek (*philarguria*) and carries the sense of avarice (greed) and miserliness.

15. The expression "food and clothing" is a synecdoche meaning that a part (food and clothing) is used to refer to the whole—food, clothing, shelter, car, etc.

16. What is meant here is coveting the wrong things.

of destruction. Notice the progression: coveting leads to entanglement; entanglement leads to plunging. What does this look like? Consider this scenario: coveting bigger profits could lead to entanglement in some shady business dealings which could lead to a plunge into prison.

This passage holds true for Christians and non-Christians alike. Greed will make you do some unimaginable and illogical things. Pray that God will free you from the inordinate love of money.

HOW TO BREAK MONEY'S VICE GRIP ON US

What is the remedy for our obsession with money? The answer is quite simple: give it away. Scripture tells us how foolish it is to hoard what we have (see Luke 12:13–21) and to be generous with our means (see Mark 12:41–44). Imagine with me as I ask some *what if* questions:

1. *What if* an employee, instead of pocketing his or her bonus, generously gave a portion (perhaps, a tenth) of it to struggling family in their neighborhood, city or to global missions?

2. *What if* a highly-paid Christian executive, instead of taking a sizable year-end bonus, fiercely advocated that all employees get a substantial bonus, helped support a local struggling family, or gave to global missions? Imagine an elephant. Instead of high-salaried executives getting the body of the elephant and the employees the tail, what if the distribution was more uniform across the company rank and file?

3. *What if* the Christian business owner charged poor customers substantially less or only what they could afford? Better yet, what if the Christian business owner (if practical) took his or her services to the poor and offered them at no charge? For example, in 48 Panera stores around St. Louis, "Customers can currently order turkey chili in a bread bowl and decide for themselves how much to pay for the item. The company has also expanded its charitable activities, which include the

day-old baked goods they have always donated to food kitchens and other charities, to include job training. Profits from Panera Care cafés go into partnerships with organizations that work with at-risk teens."[17]

4. *What if* the Christian business owner was not in business just to make money, but also to use his or her business as a means to serve others as God has graciously served him or her? For instance, what if he took a portion of his profits to help others with their debt relief?

Of course, I cannot possibly cover every scenario, but I hope two things are clear. First, my decision or indecision to be generous affects not only my immediate family but the entire human family. Mark Gornik made an important observation during his lecture on the topic "Seek the Peace of the City: Ministry in an Urban Context" at the Spring 2006 Francis Schaeffer Lecture Series.[18] He remarked that, "as the city goes, so goes the suburbs." I would amend his assertion slightly to, "as the city goes, so goes the surrounding metropolitan area." In other words, our distance from the city does not exempt us from the troubles of the city because troubles will gladly travel. Second, God has called His people to break money's vice grip on us by giving it away generously. Consider the remarkable example of the early church in Acts 2:42–47. Church members were selling possessions so that the material and real needs of others might be met. This is not a demand to sell your SUV or home; rather, this passage wonderfully illustrates how we should lightly hold our possessions and how we should be generous with our time, money, resources, and networks.

17. http://www.nationaljournal.com/next-economy/solutions-bank/the-panera-model-how-to-do-good-and-make-money-at-the-same-time-20130613.

18. The Francis Schaeffer Institute is located on the campus of Covenant Theological Seminary. Mark Gornik is Director of the City Seminary of New York and author of *To Live In Peace: Biblical Faith* and *The Changing Inner City.*

REASONS WE DON'T USE OUR INFLUENCE

There are several reasons we choose not to be salt and light in the workplace. I will address four briefly and a fifth in more depth.

Fatalism. I remember making my way through a security check at the St. Louis Airport when I said in frustration, "Traveling is so difficult." A TSA worker piped up and said, "It's because of the terrorists, and it's going to get worse before it gets better." Thinking from a salt-and-light perspective, I replied, "But we can push back the impact and effects of evil." The TSA worker, who I later discovered was in seminary, responded, "This world is too far gone; there's no use." Unfortunately, this TSA worker is indicative of many Christians who believe the world in general and the workplace in particular is so corrupt that we are left with no other option but to throw up our hands and say what's the use? That's sounds defeatist or fatalistic to my ears. In the disciples' model prayer, Jesus instructs us to pray, "Your kingdom come, your will be done on earth as it is in heaven." This petition is cosmic in scale and asks God to make what is true in heaven a reality on earth—in our workplaces here and now—through His human instruments—you and me! Daniel and his friends certainly understood this concept. Yes, they were given pagan names and were trained in the Babylonian educational system, but they settled down and sought to advance the rule of God in Babylon. In other words, they were not fatalistic, and God rewarded their faith by promoting them.

Fear. If God is sovereign, why are we so fearful to stand up for truth and what is right? Perhaps we are fearful because we fear losing the argument. God is not calling us to win a knockdown, drag-out argument; He is calling us to live faithfully and engage in rational conversation with our fellow employees. Perhaps we are fearful because we fear incurring some form of bodily harm or other forms of persecution. Perhaps we are fearful because we fear being tainted or worldly. Turner offers us help here when he explains, "We become worldly not by engaging with the world but by allowing it to shape our thinking."[19] Dear Christian, read 1 John 4:4 and Matthew 10:28. And aren't we more than conquerors?

Succumbed to the private-versus-public separation. Because of our increasingly religiously pluralistic society, Christians are being asked to "put a sock in it." In other words, we have been issued a gag order. Our secular culture has issued this decree: "Keep your religious convictions to yourself, thank you very much." Consider this quote from the late Christopher Reeves who told a student group at Yale University, " . . . in the debate over embryonic stem cell research, when matters of public policy are debated, no religions should have a seat at the table."[20] Our faith is a public faith. Our faith is meant to change how we live, play, and work; our faith is meant to inform how we think about and treat human beings. We must find a way to resume our seat at the table.

Suffering from forgetfulness. We have forgotten that we are pilgrims and this is not our home. We are not to get too comfortable on earth but to offer our bodies continually to God for his bidding. This means nothing less than allowing God to use us in whatever way He deems fit to advance His kingdom.

The Fifth Reason

The fifth reason we choose not to be salt and light in the workplace is that we have been overwhelmed and overtaken by two semi-trailer trucks: *postmodernism and secularism*.

I wonder if this has happened to you. Often when I drive on the highway to visit family and friends, I am being trailed by eighteen-wheelers. When I peer into my rear-view mirror, it appears as though these huge trucks are not only gaining on me but have overtaken me. Secularism and postmodernism are like two eighteen-wheeler trucks. They have not only gained on us, but

19. Turner, 43.

20. Pearcey, *Total Truth*, 22.

in many ways have overtaken us. Postmodernism is like the fuel for secularism. Secularism deals with our behavior and actions (something we *do*) while postmodernism (something we *think*) is an ideology prevalent in our culture. Remember the TV game show "Truth or Consequences"? A conference borrowed this name and rephrased it as "Truth *and* Consequences," with the idea that true and false ideas have real consequences. History is replete with the consequences of false ideas.[21] As Christians, let's live out the truth spelled out in God's word and thereby produce good consequences.

POSTMODERNISM

Postmodernism refers to an intellectual mood and a plethora of cultural expressions that challenge the ideals, principles, and values that lay at the core of the *modern*[22] mindset. Postmodernism touts the absurdity of absolute truth and the certainty of knowing. Postmodernism is best summed up in a response from a Christian teenager who was asked to give feedback to a speaker's weeklong teaching on the theme of loving God with all our heart, soul, and mind. The students were asked to consider the claims of Jesus (especially John 14:6), and this particular Christian teenager said, "We like his stories, but that's his truth. I don't want to judge him,

21. There are so many awful ideas resulting in horrific consequences in world history that it is hardly worth mentioning. But consider the United States' and Hitler's idea of creating a master race; consider the Rwanda Massacre (dubbed the African Holocaust) in 199. And who can forget September 11, 2001?

22. Modernism is another intellectual mood that reached its zenith in the 18th century known as the Enlightenment. Modernism espoused a rejection of knowing objective truth by a personal relationship with God, which leads to a rejection of God as a transcendent reality and of the supernatural. Truth is known objectively only through science and reason. Reason sits upon the throne. Primary in importance among the "enlightened" was the rights of man. Moderns were activists, certain, optimistic and self-confident; postmoderns are passive, uncertain, cynical, and insecure.

but I have a different truth."[23] Every person has been affected by postmodernism; it is the air we breathe.

In sum, what are the major tenets of postmodernism? First, there are no universal truths. There is very little we can agree on that is universally true for everyone, because there are many stories to live by. This makes room for two insidious ideas: tolerance and moral relativism.

Tolerance—"the highest truth"[24]—says to turn a blind eye to the corrosive nature of secular or ungodly living and values. It is a laissez-faire, 'live and let live' posture. Like laissez-faire capitalism which depends on individual rights, a laissez-faire lifestyle depends on exercising one's individual rights. Moral relativism says, "what's right for you is right for you; I define *my* right differently." Refer to the statement above by the teenager: "I have a different truth." A moral relativist says, "I live by my set of morals; you live by your set of morals."

Second, this culture is suspicious of authority primarily because of rampant abuse of authority and power in private and public arenas. A child first learns about authority within their family. What happens to that understanding of authority when mom and dad divorce or when one parent abandons the family?

Third, subjectivity trumps objectivity. "If it feels good, it must be right." Living subjectively gives me more personal freedom to do as I darn well please—no moral guilt and no moral accountability. The statement, "I am not a sinner but a victim," captures this idea of no moral guilt, which goes in hand with our therapeutic culture. Our therapeutic culture with its emphasis on self-esteem and wanting rah-rah sermons has placed a gag order on preachers. Preachers are encouraged not to say the "s-word" (sin) but rather to make people feel warm and fuzzy. Our culture's emphasis on therapeutic messages and sermons means we are hearing sermons on sin less and less. I remember a pastor telling the story of his

23. McDowell, "True for You but Not True for Me," *YouthWorker Journal,* January/February 2006, 28.

24. Neuhaus, "To Say Jesus is Lord," *First Things,* Nov. 2000, Number 107, 69–70. This is not espoused by Neuhaus but simply quoted by him.

church administrator receiving a voicemail asking, "Do you guys talk about sin out there?"

I saw these trends playing out in a conversation with a lady I met at the local Laundromat. The lady was a white, divorced mother of two. School was canceled because of inclement weather, which made driving school busses quite hazardous, so her kids accompanied her to the Laundromat. Sadly, she said the kids' father is remarried and has nothing to do with them (which is all too common these days— Christian men washing their hands of their children and abdicating their role as father). She went on to tell me that she left her church "because they did not talk about sin." She left because sin was not seriously considered and discussed.

Finally, whether you want to admit it or not, or whether you are even aware of it, you are impacted by postmodernism. Consider these statements we all have thought or perhaps made:

- "If it doesn't affect me directly, so I don't care what you do."

- "I don't know what is true anymore."

- The shotgun loaded question, "Don't you want me to be happy?"

- "Good Hindus and Buddhists will go to heaven."

- "What's right (true) for you is okay; this is right (true) for me."

- "I have no right to judge."

If you have uttered these statements or even thought them, then the corrosive ideals of postmodernism have crept into your worldview or thinking.

I have been taught to affirm the good of cultural artifacts and postmodernism is no different. So to be fair, postmodernism does tout some good tenets too.

- With unprecedented religious pluralism, we are experiencing a plethora of ideas from different cultures. Postmoderns share a sincere sensitivity for other cultures. This probably explains why my son's generation has fewer hang-ups with race than my generation or my parents' generation. They desire to see equality among genders and an acceptance of others (e.g., homosexuals). Postmodernism promotes a willingness to try and experience new things. In other words, multiculturalism is a big hit in this era. Once taboo and outlawed, interracial and interethnic couples are becoming more commonplace.

- There is a great emphasis on trying to understand and listen to others' stories. Postmoderns not only love stories but desire to experience the stories of others. This is a feeling and subjective generation. Many today desire to be honest and open and are willing to talk about their brokenness in excruciating detail. "Be transparent" is a big value for this generation. Check out some blogs or Facebook pages and notice how, without blushing, people spill their guts to virtual strangers. You might have heard young people say, "I feel you."

- There is a desperate longing for connectedness and an emphasis on community. There is an earnest desire for authenticity and a repulsion to hypocrisy. In fact, my good friend Margie Haack[25] says that the postmodern credo is "hypocrisy rots, authenticity rules."

- Those in this generation believe that truth can be known by other means besides rationalism which is often viewed as being harsh, rigid, cold, and without consideration of real feelings. This generation questions and does not automatically accept things based upon authority of the office.

The wise Christian must be skilled at sorting through what is helpful in ideological systems and what is harmful. In other words, we are called to be critical and discerning thinkers.

---

25. Margie Haack and her husband Denis Haack, lead a fine ministry called Ransom Fellowship. I strongly encourage you to check out their website www.ransomfellowship.org and subscribe to receive *Critique* Magazine and *Notes from Toad Hall.* You will not regret it.

Secularism

The word secular comes from the Latin *saeculum*. At one time the word meant "this age" or "this time here and now;" now of course it means ungodly or nonreligious. You have heard social scientists say, "The United States is becoming secularized." Secularism in the United States' moral infrastructure is like termites in a house. Termites are not only inconspicuous and stealthy but they are relentless in nibbling away at wood behind dry wall, wood underneath carpets, and hidden wooden beams that provide structural support. Termites can compromise the structural integrity of a home.

Secularism likewise is nibbling away at the moral integrity of the United States. Universal values once embraced and promulgated have given way to a "live and let live" culture. Consider this comment by Leon Kass, " . . . changes in the broader culture make it now vastly more difficult to express a common and respectful understanding of sexuality, procreation, nascent life, family . . . twenty-five years ago, abortion was still largely illegal and thought to be immoral . . . [but] today, defenders of stable, monogamous marriage risk charges of giving offense to those adults who are living in new family forms . . . Today, one must . . . apologize for voicing opinions that twenty-five years ago were nearly universally regarded as the core of our culture's wisdom on these matters."[26] While this is a fairly dated quote, it is still very relevant today. This means of course that our starting point with conversations and assumptions will be quite different now. For instance, we need to listen well and not assume people are using words the same way we are.

Secularists commend us for having religious convictions but they would rather we keep them private. Said another way, secularists want us to "just keep our mouths shut" about what we believe. Again, the late Christopher Reeves conveyed this attitude in his speech to a student group at Yale University, ". . . in the debate over

---

26. Kass, *The Wisdom of Repugnance*, The New Republic, June 2, 1997.

embryonic stem cell research, when matters of public policy are debated, no religions should have a seat at the table."[27]

In essence, secularists want us to live a double life. Live your Christian life in private and live as nominal or benign Christians in public. In other words, keep your life compartmentalized—your Christian beliefs dare not influence your public life—just conform to the status quo and don't rock the boat. However, there's a huge problem. Jesus and Paul spent time in the synagogue, but they are also spent quite a bit of time illustrating how one's personal convictions play out in the public square. In other words, Jesus and Paul spent time in the synagogue and the streets. Our Christian faith is a public faith. And aren't we supposed to model Christ's life? There is yet another problem with living a double life—hypocrisy. Hypocrisy is ugly at all times and in all places.

IMPLICATIONS OF THIS HISTORICAL MOMENT

Secularism and postmodernism describe our historical moment. But why did I bother with covering secularism and postmodernism?

First, every Christian is impacted by postmodernism and secularism. The high rate of divorce among Christians is one unfortunate result of this impact. Again, remember that postmodernism says there is no such thing as absolute truth. Appropriating this tenet means that marriage as a lifelong commitment is absurd, even for the evangelical Christian. So, for many Christians unBiblical divorce is a legitimate alternative.

So, all Christians who desire to be salt and light in the unique culture of their workplace must commit themselves to participating in a reorientation. Eugene Peterson's translation of the Apostle Paul's words in Romans 12:1–2 captures this idea well:

". . . don't become so well-adjusted to your culture (both the wider culture and your work culture) that you fit into it without even thinking. Instead, fix your attention on God. You'll be changed from the inside out. Readily recognize what he wants from you,

27. Pearcey, *Total Truth*, 22.

and quickly respond to it. Unlike the culture around you, always dragging you down to its level of immaturity, God brings the best out of you, develops well-formed maturity in you."[28]

This reorientation to maturity happens when we persistently engage in renewing our minds. We renew our minds by reading and meditating on God's word.

Second, having an awareness of postmodernism and secularism serves as a sober reminder that you may think you are communicating clearly with your coworker or boss, but you may not be. Your coworker or boss has a particular worldview that may be very different from yours, which means of course that you may be offensive and oblivious to it. You may need to be very patient and take the time to build real friendships with your coworkers before you earn the right to speak truth. We earn the right by doing our jobs with excellence, adhering to the allotted time for lunch, arriving to work on time, and working our shift. By doing so, we live out the truth before our coworkers.

CHRISTIANS WITH NO INFLUENCE

How does salt lose its saltiness? What does it mean to hide our light under a basket? Jesus is not giving us a chemistry lesson, nor is he mincing words. Salt does not lose its salinity. And it would be foolish to put a lit lamp under a clothes basket. Jesus is saying a Christian that has no influence in the workplace is like useless salt that is thrown out. And the believer who is a closet Christian at work is likened to a person who foolishly lights a lamp and tucks it away under a bushel. To put it plainly, Jesus is saying those Christians who don't use their influence in the workplace are actually living an oxymoronic existence. It doesn't compute, because Christians have the truth and are bearers of the truth in word and deed!

---

28. Peterson, *The Message*, 2052.

Apologetics in the Workplace

Notice carefully what Jesus says in Matthew 5:16. The Greek word translated as "see" suggests a person who is a position to serve as an eyewitness. When we live salty and light-filled lives in the workplace, others will witness or see our good works and give God our Father praise. Our salty and light-filled lives will serve as proof or as a defense that God exists. Our salty and light-filled lives lived out in the workplace serve as an apologetic! Imagine that. There is more at stake than receiving a paycheck; the glory and praise of God's name is at stake.

SOME FINAL WORDS AND A PRAYER

Another Vocation

Not only are we called to walk uprightly before God, to honor God through loving relationships, and to excel in our specific work; we are also called to be salt and light in the workplace. That makes four vocations! To be a disciple of Christ means to be salt and light.

A Salty and Light-filled Future

Dr. Bryan Chapell, former President of Covenant Theological Seminary, would often say that gospel work is generational, meaning parents, pastors, and teachers should be devoted to teaching our kids about God's word so that they may be salt and light in the workplace in the future. We need to be committed to Deuteronomy 6:4–7. This passage, known as the *Shema*, commands parents to teach their kids God's laws and ways.

The person with the primary role of teaching the children God's statutes was the father, as recorded in the Samuel Friedland Lectures: "Originally, responsibility for educating the child revolved completely upon the father. The Talmud states that among the obligations of the father are to teach his son Torah

(Old Testament) and teach him a livelihood (a skill, etc.)."[29] This passage also reminds us that just like we burn data onto a CD, fathers are to burn God's word on their kids' hearts and minds by talking about it when they wake up, as they drive along the road, as they walk in the park, and when they eat. Does this sounds like incessant overkill? Sure it does, and that's the point. As the primary moral educators of our kids, we need to be diligent and relentless in teaching them God's laws. Why? Because our world is diligent and relentless in indoctrinating them in attractive alternatives. As we teach them, we can also steer them into industries that are suffering a severe drought of salty, light-filled Christians, including the entertainment industry, sports, and politics.

Before concluding with a prayer for you, let me offer two final thoughts.

FIRST WORD: LEARNING FROM UBUNTUISM[30]

Nobel Laureate Desmond Tutu was asked to explain the meaning of *ubuntu* in English. He replied that there was no word in the English language that could be used to explain its meaning, but offered the following definition:

> Ubuntu is the essence of being a person. It means that we are people through other people. We cannot be fully human alone. We are made for interdependence; we are made for family.

There are three *ubuntu* principles: spirituality, consensus building, and dialogue in adult and workplace learning. When the principle of spirituality is applied, and practiced in the workplace, it changes " . . . the radical nature of work. People begin to look for the meaning beyond the economic earnings in their work."[31]

29. The Samuel Friedland Lectures, 1967–1974, The Jewish Theological Seminary of America, 15.

30. Nafukho, *Ubuntuism: An African Social Philosophy Relevant to Adult Learning and Workplace Learning*, Kathleen King and Victor C. X. Wang, Comparative Adult Education Around the Globe, 63.

31. Nafukho, 66.

Now just imagine with me a different workplace culture. What if we—brothers and sisters in Christ—were to apply not a generic spirituality but our Christian spirituality in the workplace? The workplace, where we expend 33% to 41% of our time, our thinking, and our energy—will undergo a radical transformation that benefits all workers. That sounds like a win-win proposition!

SECOND WORD: DON'T GROW WEARY

The Apostle Paul tells the church at Galatia, "Let us not become weary in doing good, for at the proper time we will reap a harvest if we do not give up. Therefore, as we have opportunity, let us do good to all people, especially to those who belong to the family of believers (Galatians 6:9–10)."

This is a call for perseverance. The agricultural motif of this passage is an apt metaphor for being salt and light in the workplace. Much like a farmer plants seeds and waits, we too are called to be salt and light in the workplace and *wait* for God to produce fruit. But here's the rub—waiting on evidence that you are making a difference can be painstakingly slow. Sometimes we may never get to see the fruit because our impact might be realized in future generations of workers rather than immediately. Remember that God does not operate by closing the deal or improving the bottom line as we measure those things. And He cannot be rushed. God works secretly, behind the scenes. This is what Jesus meant when He compared the Kingdom of God to a mustard seed in Matthew 13:31–32. The impact of God working through us to be salt and light in our workplaces will appear at first small and insignificant, like the humble beginnings of the tiny and inconspicuous mustard seed. But Jesus says that the mustard seed will grow to the size of a tree. Actually, when full grown a mustard seed plant is more like a large bush than a tree. Jesus is employing a figure of speech called hyperbole to emphasize his point—it may appear that being salt and light on your job is insignificant, but one day the impact will be amazingly and overwhelmingly evident! So, don't grow weary!

MY PRAYER FOR YOU

I worked in corporate America for over fifteen years, so I know firsthand the joys and lows of this "dog eat dog" culture. So, let me conclude with a prayer for you:

> Dear Lord, as David and Solomon prayed, " . . . there is no God like you in heaven above or on earth beneath, keeping covenant and showing steadfast love to your servants who walk before you with all their heart." You have been faithful to us when we were not faithful to you. Lord, we want to do what pleases you. We want to bring your name glory. Give us an insatiable appetite for your word, which is a lamp unto our feet and light unto our pathway. Teach us to walk before you with all our hearts in the workplace. Teach us to be courageous salty and light-filled Christians in our workplaces. In Jesus' mighty and glorious name, Amen!

DISCUSSION QUESTIONS:

1. I recently moved from Kansas City to St. Louis. While there were many advantages to this move, my biggest regret has been being away from family and college friends. Why? Because we were made for community. Have you seen this need for community in your own life?

2. As an employee, manager, or self-employed person, how were you challenged by this chapter?

3. What challenges do you have to teaching your children God's word?

4. How have you compromised your faith in the workplace? If yes, what steps might you take so that history is not repeated? If no, what advice would you share with others?

5. Can you see evidence in your life of embracing the good and bad tenets of postmodernism and the resulting secular-like lifestyle?

6. What's the potential danger of simply taking the pastor's sermon at face value without doing a careful study of the Scriptures yourself?

7. How can I use my business as a means to minister to others?

8. Compare Jesus' encounter with the rich young ruler (Luke 18:18–30) with Jesus' encounter with Zacchaeus (Luke 19:1–10). How are these passages similar and dissimilar?

9. Do you agree with Mark Gornik's assertion that "as the city goes, so goes the suburbs"?

OTHER IDEAS

Watch the films *Jungle Fever* (1991) and *Office Space* (1999) and then discuss. If you worked in these workplaces, what would it look like for you to be salt and light? What would be your responsibility if you knew Milton was treated this way?

PART 2

The Details

3

Creation: Simply Breathtaking!

"A Theater of God's Glory"

—John Calvin

During my days as a process/product engineer, I regularly inspected the quality of products produced by an intricate manufacturing process. I remember one particularly challenging product that was the size of your pinkie fingernail and as thin as two pieces of paper. This miniature part was quite the challenge. In contrast, the largest product or project I had the privilege of overseeing was an avionics test bed (ATB)—a flying laboratory. The ATB was an older military fighter fitted with new electronics. This allowed us to test the new electronics on an older jet with less risk before installing those electronics on newer aircraft.

I was responsible for the integration of several electronic boxes on this test aircraft. The process to manufacture that miniature part or to integrate several electronic boxes consisted of a series of carefully ordered steps conducted by skilled union workers. If the worker followed the process exactly, the result was usually a high-quality product. Of course, I am oversimplifying because the quality of the finished product was also related to several other factors including the quality of the raw materials, the experience of the union worker, and unpredictability of the chemicals employed.

God—the consummate process-product engineer—followed a systematic and intentional process to create our world. Naturally God is quite skilled and qualified at what He does. After following His own process, God inspected His creative acts and rendered a quality rating in Genesis 1:31a: "And God saw everything He had made, and behold, it was *very good* (italics mine)." God declared everything He had made as "very good," including mankind. All that God created was free of defects and worked as designed. God created[1] a shared habitat for many inhabitants—insects, rodents, vegetation, animals and humans. After a six-day workweek, God kicked up His heels and rested.

COMMON REVELATION

Scripture affirms that creation—the visible and invisible—reveals something about God—the Creator. This is called universal or common revelation because all human beings "hear" an inaudible message or see a display of revelation in every place, at all times, and in a universal language. King David, poet and musician, records in Psalm 19:1–4a:

> The heavens declare the glory of God;
>   the skies proclaim the work of his hands.
> Day after day they pour forth speech;
>   night after night they reveal knowledge.
> They have no speech, they use no words;
>   no sound is heard from them.
> Yet their voice goes out into all the earth,
>   their words to the ends of the world.

---

1. This word for create *(bara)* is used only when God is the subject.

Understanding verse 1 is the key to understanding this passage. In particular, what does the psalmist mean by "the heavens"? Often in Hebrew poetry, we find the use of parallelism, a restatement of what has been said previously. In other words, "heavens" and "sky above" are synonymous terms. The word "heavens" and its synonym "sky" are used as wholes to represent the individual parts. King David is saying that those things that populate the sky—namely, the sun, moon, and stars—declare the splendor, beauty, orderliness, creativity, might, magnificence and glory of God. In other words, we know something of the Creator by the creation. By asking a few interrogative questions of the text, we can better soak in the significance of verses 2 to 4a:

- How often is this message heard? Around the clock—from day to day, and from night to night (verse 2).

- Is an interpreter needed? No, because this language is understood by all peoples on the earth (verse 3).

- What is the geographical reach of this message? Throughout all the earth (verse 4a). This is why Paul can write in Romans 1:20 that mankind is without excuse, because every man everywhere and at all times hears a message courtesy of God's creation, which publicly discloses the truth of God's eternal power and divine nature (Romans 1:20).

Of course, sin has severely damaged the world (more about this in the next chapter), but imagine the original pristine glory and sparkle of God's creation before the fall of man! Think about your first bicycle or first automobile; it sparkled because it recently rolled off the assembly line. Man's missteps leading to the fall have caused our world to groan for liberation from decay and bondage as Paul reminds us in Romans 8:18–25. Yet, the creation still reflects God's glory, and it's always on display. According to Eugene Peterson, John Calvin, the prolific and courageous reformer headquartered in Geneva, "frequently referred to the world around us as a 'theater of God's glory.'"[2] Every day we are treated to a new, no-cost theatrical scene that showcases God's glory! And sometimes,

2. Peterson, *The Contemplative Pastor*, 68.

God showcases something extra when He allows us to witness a lunar eclipse with our naked eye or a meteor shower using a high magnification microscope. My prayer for myself is to slow down occasionally and behold what's playing on God's big screen. I hope that is your prayer too.

PURPOSE: "IT'S IN THERE"

Years ago, television advertisers developed a famous commercial jingle for Ragu Spaghetti sauce—"it's in there." This slogan meant that the sauce contained all the necessary constituent ingredients that qualified it as ready-to-use without the need to add something else. Ragu Spaghetti sauce was fully equipped as designed. In like manner, God has built in a purpose for every created entity. Sunlight is used not only for photosynthesis but also determines the seasons. Even that pesky and annoying honeybee has a purpose. My son's seventh-grade science teacher is also a beekeeper, so I asked him this question:

> Mr. Science Teacher,
>   A quick question—is there an interdependency between bees collecting nectar from flowers and the health of the shrub? Can you help me with this?
>   Thanks.

Here is his reply:

> Hi Mr. Bobo,
>   Some plants need honeybees to properly pollinate the flowers so that they will produce seeds. If the flowers are not thoroughly pollinated, then the plant will not produce enough seed to ensure that it will propagate. Seeds are like a lot of things in nature. [It] takes thousands of them to ensure that maybe 1–2 survive, so the fewer seeds produced, the lower the chance new plants will be produced, with an even lower likelihood of the plant passing its genetic traits on to its offspring. Thus, the fewer seeds produced, the fewer offspring . . . not to mention that the parent plant is not getting any younger!

If no seeds sprout to replace the parent plant, then the plant hasn't done its job properly.

Now, we can also look at this question in another way. If bees don't collect nectar from the plant, then maybe the plant is not healthy. Assuming it is a species of plant that bees regularly visit to collect nectar from, then it may be that something is wrong. It could mean there is a health problem with the plant, or one of several other things. Sometimes other nectar sources are more attractive to the honeybees, so they may frequent the plant less often. Honeybees tend to know when something is just not quite right.

Like bees, human beings also have an intrinsic purpose. Human beings have incredible value and worth because they were created in the image of God (*imago Dei*). We image God by working. And to use the Ragu jingle, "it's in there." We have the constituent ingredients *to engage in meaningful work.* One of the duties God gave to mankind—males and females—was to "fill the earth and subdue it" and to "have dominion over" the animal kingdom and all the earth. [3]

Subdue "comes from the root that means 'to knead' or 'to tread' and refers to bringing the earth under cultivation so that the race could multiply."[4] In other words, Adam and Eve were to don hard hats and develop the land. They were called to make the land livable and civilized. To make livable means to create things like language, music, computers, washing machines, cell phones, and constitutions. God shares His sovereign rule with human beings to make our world livable (not so we can abuse our dominion). Albert Wolters sums it up best when he writes, "People must now carry on the work of development: by being fruitful they must fill it

---

3. The phrases "fill the earth and subdue it" and "have dominion over" are taken from Genesis 1:26–28. This passage is commonly referred to as the cultural mandate. Adam demonstrates his dominion by naming the animals in Genesis 2.

4. Ryrie, *Basic Theology*, 232.

even more; by subduing it they must form it even more. Mankind, as God's representatives on earth, carries on where God left off."[5]

To have dominion over means to rule or manage the animal kingdom righteously. Again, we do not manage from a position of superiority or abuse, but in humility. As such, Christians should support those who fight for animal rights. We should be appalled at those who abuse animals. On the other hand, we must also cry foul when some animals are treated far better than the human beings that care for them.

STEWARDS

Another duty or divine assignment that God gave to mankind was to care for the garden (Genesis 2:15). I remember a dear sister in Christ who believed that work is a curse and therefore a result of the fall of man. Actually, it is not. God called Adam and Eve to work and keep the garden before that history-altering chapter, Genesis 3. Adam and Eve were given an assignment. The Hebrew word for "keep"[6] means to "have charge of"; in other words, Adam and Eve were to act as stewards over God's garden. A steward cares for what belongs to another. In stewarding the garden, Adam and Eve were essentially "subduing the earth" (Genesis 1:28). Because the sovereign God assigned the work, there is dignity and value in it. And because we are significant as God's image bearers, everything we do is significant.

I often told my students at Lindenwood University that God entrusted to them the privilege and opportunity to attend college. They are fundamentally stewards of a trust, and God is truly their professor. And as such, I reminded them, they should care for their trust with excellence. I frequently quoted Colossians 3:22–23:

> 22 Slaves, obey your earthly masters in everything; and
> do it, not only when their eye is on you and to curry their

5. Wolters, *Creation Regained*, 36.

6. This word sounds like *shamar* in Hebrew. Dr. Calvin DeWitt, professor of Environmental Studies at the University of Wisconsin, helped me with this concept when he delivered Francis Schaeffer Lectures on caring for the earth.

favor, but with sincerity of heart and reverence for the
Lord. 23 Whatever you do, work at it with all your heart,
as working for the Lord, not for human masters.

The Apostle Paul encouraged slaves in the church at Colossae
to do their work not to earn brownie points with their earthly masters but rather to do their work as if it was for the Lord. Whatever
we do, we are called to do it with zeal and excellence as unto the
Lord—our true boss. All that we do—work, live, play—all come
under the supervision or lordship of Christ. In the end, *whatever
we do*, we're doing it for Christ.

DISCUSSION QUESTIONS:

1. As a steward, God has entrusted to you your job/vocation.
   Was that a new concept for you?

2. At a Francis Schaeffer Lecture series on stewarding creation,
   I remember Dr. Cal DeWitt saying that he instructed his students go to a forest, lie down, and listen to the leaves falling
   to the earth. Eccentric? I don't think so. Dr. DeWitt was attempting to get his students to slow down and behold God's
   creation. When was the last time you took the time to do that?

4

Sin, Consequences, and our Work

"Evil runs through everything . . .."

—CORNELIUS PLANTINGA, JR.

Dr. Charles C. Ryrie called the fall of man, "the darkest hour of all human history."[1] At the fall, something went awfully and terribly wrong. An intruder invaded God's creation and ushered in brokenness on a cosmic scale!

The Apostle Paul writes in Romans 5:12, "Therefore, just as sin entered the world through one man, and death through sin, and in this way death came to all people, because all sinned." Captured succinctly in this verse is the far-reaching scope of sin: it came into the whole world. Here world is from the Greek word *kosmos*. The effects of sin reach not only the earth, but the universe and beyond. Every inch of God's universe is tainted by sin. The damning effects of sin are cosmic in scope and cataclysmic in depth. The cosmic

1. Ryrie, *Basic Theology*, 236.

64

scope of sin is captured in the last three lines of the third stanza of *Joy to the World*:

> No more let sins and sorrows grow,
> Nor thorns infest the ground;
> He comes to make His blessings flow
> Far as the curse is found,
> Far as the curse is found,
> Far as, far as, the curse is found.[2]

The effects of sin extend as far as the curse is found. Yet God also wants to use us to extend His blessings as far as the curse is found.

The cataclysmic depth of sin included both spiritual and physical death to all men. When Adam, our representative, sinned we all sinned. This discussion comes under the more technical term of the imputation[3] of Adam's sin, which is beyond the scope of this work. However, we may illustrate the doctrine of imputation this way.

- As my representative, Adam acted on my behalf. His actions had far-reaching negative consequences—namely, all men sinned, all men stand condemned before a holy and just God, and all men are sentenced to death (eternal separation from God). Consider these other *negative* consequences that I refer to as estrangements:[4]

  - Man is estranged from God. This is what the Bible means when it says we are dead in our trespasses. Because of

2. Dr. Michael Williams, professor at Covenant Theological Seminary, has written *Far As The Curse is Found: The Covenant Story of Redemption*. I received the content of this book from Dr. Williams' Covenant Theology course lectures. The material was so foreign to me that it took a year for me to grasp the beauty of the content.

3. Read carefully Romans 5:12–21. I also recommend a very scholarly work by John Murray, *Imputation of Adam's Sin*.

4. Adapted from Dr. Francis Schaeffer's five separations. Schaeffer spoke of five separations: man is separated from God; man is separated from man; man is separated from himself; man is separated from the animal kingdom; and man is separated from creation. For more, see Dr. Schaeffer's *Genesis in Space and Time: The Flow of Biblical History*.

Adam's sin, all human beings are estranged from God even while in their mother's womb.

- Man is estranged from man. This is why men have a low regard for men. This is why men murder men; this is why men abuse women; this is why men fly planes into buildings.

- Man is estranged from creation. This is why mankind abuses the environment.

- Man is estranged from the animal kingdom. This is why mankind abuses animals.

- Man is estranged from himself. Men don't know who they are; so this is why we all need a psychiatrist!

- Man is estranged from his work. Man either devalues work or makes work an idol or considers some work more valuable than other forms of work.

- Similarly, as my representative, Christ (the second Adam), acted on my behalf and His actions had far reaching *positive* consequences—namely, for those in Christ,[5] all are declared righteous (the sentence of death is lifted; we are exonerated), and all in Christ are birthed to new[6] life.

- Just as I receive benefits (or perks) because of what Christ did on my behalf, I also receive demerits (or curses) because of what Adam did on my behalf. Yet Paul reminds us that the free gift of God (Christ's imputed righteousness) is vastly and profoundly different from Adam's one trespass.

5. "In Christ" is Paul's expression for those who are saved. Others refer to this as a mystical union between Christ and us.

6. The word translated as "new" is *kainos* in Greek; it means either new in kind or new in quality. Here it means new in kind or new in the sense of being superior in kind to the old (as in 2 Corinthians 5:17).

A RIGHTEOUS ACT FOR A HEINOUS ACT

In July 2005 I visited a village near Cape Town, South Africa called Masiphumele, which means "success." In this township, a village leader with the AIDS virus was having sex with young girls. Worse still, neither the girls nor this leader would come forward for treatment because it is taboo to disclose such information. This leader's one act was so unrighteous and heinous that as a consequence every member of this small community suffers—even the unborn.

I would love to see your face after reading about this egregious violation. What is your reaction to this awful injustice? Are you appalled? Angry? Disgusted? Incensed? Are you beside yourself? Is your blood boiling? Do you recoil from the disgust? If you answered yes to these questions (and I hope you did) then welcome to God's world. Not only does this prove you are aware of sin's disgusting ugliness but you have just gotten a taste of God's reaction to Adam's sin and our sin.[7] The effects of this heinous sin would live on for generations in this small village. This is a microcosm of how Adam's sin impacted the world from his day to our own.

Now, imagine a new leader comes to this small village and acts radically unlike his predecessor's heinous act that it has the impact of erasing the consequences of past damage. Imagine his action condemns his predecessor, puts him in jail, and gets treatment for those affected by AIDS. Unlike the result from the first leader, the result of this new leader's righteous action benefits everyone in the village (including the unborn).

---

7. I remember passionately telling my Lindenwood University class of youth-ministers-in-training that God hates sin. Hating sin means at least three things: (1) you are quick to seek forgiveness with God because you know what our sin cost God—His Son "pinned naked to the cross of pain and shame" (See Dr. David Chapman's article, "Deep is the Saving Wisdom of God" in Covenant Magazine, Spring 2008 issue, pp. 16–17); (2) you will be swift, gentle, prayerful, and discerning to lovingly confront a brother and sister in Christ about his/her sin; and (3) our church leaders will be swift, gentle, prayerful, and discerning in lovingly carrying out church discipline. Carrying out implications (2) and (3) is never easy, always uncomfortable, and never done perfectly, but God gives us guidelines in His word for exercising discipline.

This is what meant is by imputation: on one hand, the negative consequences of Adam's sin—his sinful nature, condemnation, and death—are imputed to us. On the other hand, the positive consequences of Christ's one act—his righteousness, justification, and eternal life—are imputed or credited to us. In other words, because of Christ's one act, we are declared righteous and justified and have been granted eternal life.

But how did we come to need this rescue? Let's review the tragic events leading to the fall of man.

PRE-FALL DIALOGUE

Satan initiates a dialogue with Eve by asking her, "Did God actually say, 'You shall not eat of any tree in the garden'?" Satan is questioning whether God will follow through on His promise that "you will surely die." Notice carefully what Eve said in response in Genesis 3:2: "We may eat fruit from the trees in the garden, but God did say, 'You must not eat fruit from the tree that is in the middle of the garden, and you must not touch it, or you will die.'" Eve added something to the original prohibition. Compare Eve's response to Genesis 2:17, "but you must not eat from the tree of the knowledge of good and evil, for when you eat from it you will certainly die."[8] Eve inserted "neither shall you touch it." In this brief exchange, Satan successfully convinced Eve to make the prohibition even more restrictive and onerous. Satan has insinuated with his line of questioning that God is an ogre who wishes to rein in the freedom of Adam and Eve. Moreover, Satan is successful in planting the idea in Eve's head that God is withholding something from her and Adam—being like God. If God were not withholding that, Eve thinks, they could live autonomously as the first humanists. Suddenly the tree of knowing good and evil becomes pleasant to the eyes and desirable for nourishment. Eve takes and eats and politely passes the fruit onto her husband, Adam.

8. A more literal translation of the original Hebrew text is "die, you will die." English versions tend to translate this repetition as "you shall surely die." God is going on record as saying "you can be sure of it."

AFTER THE FALL: DEFORMITY AND DECAY

Officially, Adam made a false step[9] and trespassed God's prohibition to forgo eating from the tree of knowing good and evil. The aftermath is catastrophic, and God metes out sentences. There is no immunity because God is just—sin must be punished.

SENTENCES METED OUT

God's intent when He made the world was that it would operate on the principle of justice because He is a God of justice. As a just God, He must keep justice and maintain order or peace. This is why God has ordained the civil authorities to maintain order by rendering justice (See Romans 13). Sitting on His throne, God as justice of the peace, convenes a trial and metes out sentences that are commensurate with the respective crimes for each of the defendants who conspired in the first gang crime.

Defendant Satan—because of his part in this crime and as a constant reminder of his defeat, the serpent is told that his mode of travel will be on his belly and he will eat dust. His seed and the woman's seed will be engaged in a constant spiritual battle. Ultimately, the woman's seed will deliver a fatal blow to Satan, while he will inflict a wound on her future male offspring. This cosmic battle recorded in Genesis 3:15 is known as the "mother promise."[10] Promised here in germ form is the anticipation of Mary being impregnated without a man's sperm. This is the first assurance of the coming Christ child who will grow in stature and favor with man and will issue a fatal blow to Satan by dying on a cross. Yes, Christ secures a victory for us by dying on a cross and subsequently being resurrected!

9. Driver and Plummer, *The International Critical Commentary on Romans*, 1:39–40.

10. Dr. Michael Williams, Professor at Covenant Seminary, is fond of saying this.

> **Defendant Eve**—because of her disobedience Eve will experience excruciating labor pains in delivering offspring. Additionally, because of her desire[11] to rule her husband or usurp his authority, there will be constant tug of war between her and her husband Adam for headship rights in the marriage.

> **Defendant Adam**—because of his disobedience, Adam will till the ground for food, yet it will not be problem or anxiety-free. He will exert much effort and be subjected to much frustration to grow greens, grapes, corn, and potatoes.

As a final penalty, Adam and Eve are escorted out the garden and posted guards forbid them from re-entering. Alas, the damage had already been done.

In the story of Dr. Jekyll and Mr. Hyde, Dr. Jekyll described what evil had done to him (resulting in his second self, Mr. Hyde) as an *"imprint of deformity and decay."*[12] Adam's one act of disobedience has left an imprint of deformity and decay on us and the entire universe.

This one act of disobedience or sin has robbed God's theater of some of its original splendor and glory and has also disrupted the peace (shalom). Yet the earth and the fullness thereof is still the Lord's. The cosmos remains God's territory. Read aloud this quote by Christopher Wright as recorded in *Critique* Magazine:

"The whole earth . . . belongs to Jesus. It belongs to him by right of creation, by right of redemption and by right of future inheritance —- as Paul affirms in the magnificent cosmic declaration of Colossians 1:15–20. 'All things' in this passage suggests that Christ is reconciling the entire universe to Himself. So, wherever we go in his name, we are walking on his property. There is not an inch of the planet that does not belong to Christ."[13]

---

11. See Genesis 4:7, Here the word for desire is the same as in Genesis 3:16. In Genesis 4:7 sin is personified and seeks to rule over Cain.

12. Stevenson, *The Strange Case of Dr. Jekyll and Mr. Hyde and Other Stories*, 79.

13. See Walking on Christ's Property, *Critique* Magazine, Year End 2007 issue, 2.

The patch of land that you trek from your car to your desk, counter, or assembly line belongs to Christ. It doesn't belong to your company; it belongs to Jesus Christ! Isn't that encouraging?

DISCUSSION QUESTIONS:

1. What or who dulls our lackluster reaction to sin?

2. What's at stake when churches don't practice biblical church discipline?

3. Case Studies (the names have been changed because these case studies are based on true accounts):

    - On a recent trip to the doctor's, I was chatting with the doctor's assistant as she took my vitals. She went on to tell me about her friend Eve, who was enamored with a pastor's voice on the radio. Not content with just hearing his melodic voice, Eve eventually attended the church to see the man behind the voice. Not content with seeing his face and hearing his voice, Eve and the pastor had an affair. This one-night stand wrecked the pastor's family and Eve's family. The full extent of the damage cannot be predicted. Yet, the doctor's aid said, "I wanted to say something, but who am I to judge?" Could this have been averted? What is our role as Christians in this case? I often hear Christians say, "do not judge" according to Matthew 7. What is the context for Jesus words in Matthew 7? Compare this passage to 1 Corinthians 11:17-34, where the Apostle Paul tells us to judge. (This may be the topic or subject of my next book–our confusion about judging.)

4. Two teenagers in the church's youth group are having sex. What is your responsibility if you are aware of this?

5

Some Marvelous Good News: Redemption!

"I am free at last, thank God Almighty, I am free at last."

—Dr. Martin Luther King, Jr.

In *Bound for Canaan: The Epic Story of the Underground Railroad, America's First Civil Rights Movement,*[1] Fergus Bordewich describes the unfortunate plight of a slave attempting to run away from a white man who brutally assaulted his wife. This excerpt is fairly long so that we get the proper context:

> Henson was born on June 15, 1789, on the eastern shore
> of Chesapeake Bay, on a farm belonging to Francis

1. Bordewich, *Bound for Canaan: The Epic Story of the Underground Railroad, America's First Civil Rights Movement,* 11–12. This is a voluminous work—believe me. It would be difficult reading if it were not for the glimpses of redemption—benevolent slave owners and Quakers—collaborating together to help slaves on to their freedom.

Newman, about a mile from Port Tobacco. His mother was the property of a neighbor, Dr. Josiah McPherson, an amiable alcoholic who treated the infant Henson as something of a pet, *bestowing* upon him his own Christian name. In accordance with common practice, McPherson hand hired out Henson's mother to Newman, to whom Henson's father belonged. Newman's overseer, a "rough, coarse man," had brutally assaulted Henson's mother. Whether this was an actual or attempted rape, or the more mundane brutality of daily life, Henson does not make clear. Perhaps, he didn't know. Whatever the cause, Henson's father, normally a good-humored man, attacked the overseer with ferocity and would have killed him, had not Henson's mother intervened. For a slave to lift his hand "against the sacred temple of a white man's body," even in self-defense, was an act of rebellion. Slaves were sometimes executed, and occasionally even castrated, for such an act. Knowing that retribution would be swift, Henson's father fled. Like most runaways, however, he didn't go far, but hid in the surrounding woods, venturing at night to beg food at nearby cabins. Eventually, hunger compelled him to surrender. Slaves from surrounding plantations were ordered to witness his punishment for their "moral improvement." One hundred lashes were laid by a local blacksmith, fifty lashes at a time. Bleeding and faint, the victim was then held up against the whipping post and his right ear fastened to it with a "tack." The blacksmith then sliced the ear off with a knife, to the sound of cheers from the crowd.

The similarities between the horrific plight of Henson's father as a slave and our plight before God's gracious rescue are bone-chilling and eerie.

- We too were the property of a ruthless, rough, coarse and brutal taskmaster—Satan.

- We were hired out to Satan and he brutally assaulted and pimped us.

- Satan's treatment of us caused us to behave "with ferocity" and carelessness.

We desperately needed a liberator. We needed someone to take us by the hand and lead us to freedom. Our liberator is none other than Jesus Christ. Jesus' death was the necessary price to win our freedom, as former slaves, from the ruthless, unrelenting, capricious slumlord, Satan. Said another way, we were held hostage by Satan and held under the bondage of sin. Our redemption was by means of a ransom. Jesus' substitutionary death satisfies the requirements of the ransom note. No matter how you slice it, redemption is solely of God's sovereign grace. We did not lift a finger to earn it or help in the transaction. Because of their willful amnesia, God constantly reminded the Israelites, "I am the Lord God who brought you out of Egypt, out of the house of slavery." This historic act serves as a vivid picture of redemption, not only for the Israelites, but for us as well.

REDEEMED FROM/TO

What do we owe a God who has acted so graciously and selflessly on our behalf? It is true we were redeemed *from* the vicious grip of Satan and his minions, but we are also redeemed *to do* something. Three authors can give us clarity on this *doing* aspect of our redemption. Mattson and Miller explain that "evangelism brings us to the Kingdom [or into the covenant family of God], but once we have entered, we must seek the purpose of being in the Kingdom."[2] After being saved, I need to roll up my sleeves and say, "God, I am reporting to duty. What can I do to advance your kingdom?" God may say, "I want you right where you are." In other words, God may be saying to stay put on that job and possess a salty and light work ethic. Or He may want you to leave your job and go when He leads. Nancy Pearcey aptly puts it this way, "Redemption is not just about being *saved from sin*, [but] it is also about being *saved to something*—to resume the task for which *we were originally created*."[3]

2. Mattson and Miller, *Finding a Job You Can Love*, 19.

3. Pearcey, *Total Truth*, 47.

The million-dollar question is what is the task for which we were originally created? We were created to be "agents of God's sovereign rule."[4] Remember chapter 3 and specifically Genesis 1:26–28? We were created to serve as God's vice-regents, regents who rule and steward God's creation righteously.

Considering what it cost God—the death of His sinless and law-abiding son—isn't ruling on God's behalf the reasonable thing to expect of us debtors? Still not convinced? Consider just one benefit that Christ's death and subsequent resurrection afforded us—forgiveness.

UNDENIABLY FORGIVEN

You are forgiven of your sins by God. God has forfeited His right to retaliate or hold a grudge against you because of Jesus' atoning work on the cross. God took out His retaliation or vengeance or anger once-and-for-all on the perfect Passover Lamb—Jesus Christ.[5] Just consider how much you have been forgiven. Consider what heinous things you think about or have even committed—things only you and God know about. You have been forgiven; these sins have been tossed as far as the east is from the west (Psalm 103:12). The integrity of God's character gives me blessed assurance that I can believe this without doubting. I may have to suffer the earthly consequences of a sin, but I am not sentenced to condemnation. This is what it means to belong to a just God.

DEBTORS

We are ultimately and unquestionably debtors. Matthew 18:21–35 makes this very clear. According to Philippians 2:1–10, Christ willingly surrendered the rights and privileges that rightly and only belonged to Him as the King of Glory. He assumed the form

---

4. Mouw, *Calvinism in the Las Vegas Airport*, 68.

5. This is the meaning of propitiation as translated in the King James Version of 1 John 2:2.

of a slave—someone with absolutely no rights—and was obedient to death on a cross. Not once did Christ say while He hung in agony and humiliation on the cross, "Hey, wait a minute, do you know who I am?" He was obedient unto death. Jesus paid off our enormous debt with His own life. We are truly debtors.

What do we owe a gracious God like this who gave up His son? The Heidelberg Confession, question and answer 1, provides us assistance with this question.

Question 1: What is your only comfort in life and death?

Answer. That I with body and soul, both in life and death, am not my own, but belong unto my faithful Savior Jesus Christ; who, with his precious blood, hath fully satisfied for all my sins, and delivered me from all the power of the devil; and so preserves me that without the will of my heavenly Father, not a hair can fall from my head; yea, that all things must be subservient to my salvation, and therefore, by his Holy Spirit, he also assures me of eternal life, and makes me sincerely willing and ready, henceforth, to live unto him.

Notice some of the indicatives (what God has done on our behalf and what is true) and imperatives (our obedience response to the indicatives) from the answer (*in italic*):

- Indicative: " . . . I with body and soul, both in life and death, am not my own, but belong unto my faithful Savior Jesus Christ; who, with his precious blood, hath *fully satisfied* for all my sins, and *delivered* me from all the power of the devil; and so *preserves* me that without the will of my heavenly Father . . ." God's anger has been fully satisfied; I have been delivered; and God preserves me.

- Imperative: " . . . and therefore, by his Holy Spirit, he also assures me of eternal life, and *makes me sincerely willing and ready, henceforth, to live unto him.*"

A clear response to the indicative of being redeemed is being "willing and ready to live unto him." Yet despite this clear imperative, we still resist. Active participation in Christian discipleship helps to transform that resistance to being agreeable and pliable for service.

GOALS OF DISCIPLESHIP

C. S. Lewis in his classic book *Mere Christianity*, asserts, "The question is not what we intended ourselves to be, but what He intended us to be when He made us."[6] Discipleship is a journey of moving toward what God intended us to be when He made us.

One goal of discipleship is to actively participate in our transformation into the image of Christ. If you carefully watch the movie *Thirteen*, you will quickly notice a transformation taking place right before your eyes. Naïve and innocent, Traci is *transformed* into the image of Eviss, a troubled, mischievous, streetwise, and overly sexed teenager. Believe it or not the similarities between Traci's transformation and the Christian's transformation[7] are striking.

Just like Traci participated in her inward transformation by practicing Eviss' ungodly practices, we participate in our inward transformation into the image of Christ by practicing spiritual disciplines like fasting, meditating, journaling, praying, and personal Bible study. And Christ has promised that what He started, He will complete (see Philippians 1:6).

Discipleship also has as its goal a reorientation of a person's thought life, heart life, and worldview. Why? Because we have been immeasurably impacted by the culture or society in which we live. I agree heartily with Jonathan J. Bonk when he writes, "The system of values which are maintained by a society have a *profound effect* upon the character of the individual members of the society (italics mine)."[8] We make choices daily, yet our choices are not always based on a Christian worldview. Often, they are based knowingly or unknowingly on other systems of values. What are these some

6. Lewis, *Mere Christianity*, 203.

7. We get our word *metamorphosis* from the Greek word.

8. Bonk, "The Historical and Cultural Context of Missionary Affluence." *Mi$$ion$ and Money: Affluence as a Western Missionary Problem*, 17.

of these systems of values? Read again Chapter 2—in particular the sections on postmodernism and secularism.

So what orientation are we born with? And what idols of our culture influence this orientation?

ORIENTATION AT BIRTH

What was our orientation at birth? In a word, we were crooked. We were born with an orientation to do evil. Genesis 6:9 describes our bent this way, "The Lord saw that the wickedness of man was great in the earth, and that every intention of the thoughts of his heart was only evil continually." Discipleship is about changing our bent or tendency from doing evil to doing good. Discipleship is chiefly about cardiology, as one friend puts it. God is changing our deceitful wicked hearts to long for Him and not for empty and worthless idols. But idols are fierce and unrelenting, and they cause us to resist us along the journey of discipleship.

What is idolatry? I like the definition Judson Cornwall gives: "Idolatry is . . . the response of personal adoration toward something less than Jehovah God, whether that something is self, an object made by ourselves, or a concept [e.g., an ideology like postmodernism] we may have embraced . . . an idol may be metal or mental, carved by man or conceived in the mind; *but its outer form is less important than the force it exerts upon our lives.*"[9]

Notice Cornwall's concluding sentence—the form is unimportant; what's important is the force or influence it exerts upon our lives. Our idols savagely beat us into submission. Idols are so relentless that they win and we pay an amazingly huge price.

IDOLS OF OUR CULTURE

Several idols of our culture vie for our allegiance, time, and service. The sway of idols is so powerful and seductive that we

9. Cornwall, *Things We Adore: How To Recognize and Get Free of Idolatry*, 18.

embarrassingly bow to worthless things as though we had been hypnotized. We foolishly think we control our idols, but actually our idols control us.

These idols work in concert to prevent us from completely loving and serving God with all our hearts, with all our soul, with all our might, and with all our mind. There are many idols vying for our allegiance but I contend that two idols have the greatest impact on our effectiveness to be salt and light in the workplace: 1) personal autonomy and 2) materialism.

Personal Autonomy

Personal autonomy has been elevated to an inalienable right in our culture. This desire for autonomy has been around a very long time. Our parents Adam and Eve wanted autonomy. Yet let me remind us where autonomy landed Adam and Eve—banished from the garden and estranged from God. Not convinced yet that autonomous living is ill advised? Perhaps you should see a psychiatrist, because William Young gives this poignant diagnosis: "Autonomy is lunacy."[10] Those who thirst for autonomy are lunatics.

Despite all the trappings and pitfalls of autonomy, we still nonetheless desperately want to live autonomously. Autonomy has become the new intoxicant in our day. Pastor John Piper writes, "We live in a time and . . . culture that is *so drunk* with the centrality of the values of men, and ourselves in particular, and our rights, and our virtues, and our esteem, that a sentence like [Romans 3:4] must land us either with absolute incomprehensibility or rage (*italics* mine)."[11] This explains why Christians and non-Christians alike find church discipline incomprehensible and simply absurd. Christian discipleship is to the Christian what rehab is for recovering alcoholic. Rehab for an alcoholic seeks to change an unhealthy affection and affinity to something that is healthier. Christian

10. Young, *The Shack*, 132.

11. Dr. John Piper on Romans 3:1–8, *Let God Be True Though Every Man a Liar.*

discipleship is moving away from ungodly addictions to being sober or back into the lap of the true lover of our souls, Jesus Christ.

Materialism

Materialism claims that my stuff defines me and my stuff gives me worth. We think that we control our idols. The reverse is true. Instead of having a grip on our stuff, our stuff has a grip on us. For those who have succumb to the lure of materialism, the accumulation of stuff becomes their excessive preoccupation.

It's hardly worth mentioning that we reside in a consumerist society. Every American Christian probably struggles with materialism although some of us have given into this more than others. Some have actually bowed the knee to the idol of materialism.

In our materialistic society, nearly everything is for sale or has been commoditized. A woman's eggs can be bought. A man's sperm can be purchased. Babies are bought on the black market. And opportunistic marketers relentlessly sell us discontent.

Consider a few messages that sell discontent:

- You will be happy if you have a new body.

- You will be happy if you buy this car or SUV.

- You will be happy if you have this title and this position at this company.

- And of course, you can only be happy if you have this home.

The challenge is that the rules or standards for achieving contentment are always in a state of flux. One moment you need this thing to make you happy, the next moment you need this person to make you happy. Scripture reminds us that naked we came into the world, naked we depart the world (see Job 1:21). Scripture also reminds us that where our hearts are, there will be our treasure too (see Luke 12:34). In other words, what we pursue is what we value.

- When are enough things enough?

- When are enough suits enough?

- When are enough shoes enough?
- When are enough hair extensions enough?
- When are enough shirts enough?
- When is enough home square footage enough?

I remember covering some of these questions in a sermon and a lady said to me afterwards, "You stepped on my toes." This discomfort pales in comparison to the pain and suffering the idols of materialism inflict on us. However, there is a remedy to idolatry. I remember reading that "an outbreak of contentment will bring our economy to its knees."[12] An outbreak of contentment will also bring us peace and release from the idol of materialism.

There is a parallel between idolatry and the collapse of Britney Spears that *Rolling Stone* magazine called "the most public downfall of *any star* in history (*italics* mine)."[13] The author of the piece, Vanessa Grigoriadis, remarked that "more than any other star today, Britney epitomizes the crucible of fame for the famous: loving it, hating it and never quite being able to stop it from destroying you." Similarly, you have a love-hate relationship with your idols—waffling between loving and hating them—but in the end you will never quite be able to stop your idols from destroying you! Our idols resemble a ruthless impersonal machine that demands more and more of our time, energy, and brainpower. Here is the plain truth:, what we worship is what we will serve religiously. The converse is also true: what we serve religiously, we will worship.

In a hilariously funny scene on the television program *The Cosby Show*, Bill Cosby was at the doctor's office. His heart is apparently being monitored, because he is asked to get on a treadmill for evaluation. With probes strategically affixed to his body, the medical attendants set the treadmill to a relatively slow speed and then gradually increase it. Initially Bill says, "This is a piece of cake," and goes on to clown a bit until he is unable to keep up with the speed of the treadmill. He eventually falls off because the speed

12. See Bonk.

13. Grigoriadis, *The Tragedy of Britney Spears*, RollingStone Magazine, February 21, 2008, 48.

was too overwhelming for him to keep pace. This funny scene describes exactly the benign-to-malignant pace or demands of our idols. They begin by making little and subtle demands, but eventually idols will make you go faster, faster and faster—thus causing you to sacrifice time with spouse, children, family, and rest.

PROPER MOTIVATION

How do we become motivated to pursue discipleship and worship God rather than idols? I find my motivation in the indicative or "already" aspects of Scripture. The indicatives of Scripture—what God has done on my behalf through the person of Jesus Christ—compel me to be actively involved in becoming what God intended me to be originally. And as I participate in the *becoming*, coworkers, neighbors, family members and even the earth itself benefit. R. T. France says it best: "Disciples, if they are true to their calling [of being salt and light], would make the earth a purer and more palatable place [to live]."[14] Christians can make their workplaces purer and more palatable places to work by being salt and light. And staying in the game of discipleship makes our salty lives saltier and our light-filled lives more luminous.

DISCUSSION QUESTIONS:

1. In light of the full breadth of what God has done on our behalf, isn't it our reasonable service to be salt and light in the workplace?

2. Idolatry. Our idols can be difficult to detect and identify because often they are good and noble things that earn us compliments: "He has a good work ethic" or "Your home is so neat and tidy." Besides the idols of personal autonomy and materialism, what are other idols in your life? (Note: to say you don't have any idols is like saying you have not sinned. And the Apostle John calls such people who say they have not

14. France, *Tyndale Commentary on Matthew*, 112.

sinned "deceived." See 1 John 1:8). Here are some questions to help you identity your idols:

3. For what or whom do you live for? We all live for someone or something.

4. In what or whom do you locate your worth and significance?

5. What or who is relentless in demanding more and more of your money, time, and energy?

6

All Things New!

"Behold, I am making all things new."

—GOD

The Apostle John relays some good news in Revelation 21:5: "Behold, I am making all things new." God promises to make all things new. In this instance, the word *new* means qualitatively new—so new that we have not experienced it before in this life. All the estrangements spoken of in Chapter 4 will be reversed. And, in the new heavens and the new earth, we will experience work in a new way. Yes, there will still be work to do in the new heavens and new earth, but it will be free of frustration, corruption, and heartache. We will do this work well as Jesus built tables and chairs without defects in Joseph's carpentry shop. We will truly do our work as unto the Lord, gladly and with great delight (see Colossians 3:23-25).

Even better, some of the work we do in this life will be welcomed into the new heavens and new earth as alluded to in Revelation 21:26: "They will bring into it [the new heavens and new earth] the glory and honor of the nations." Counted in "the glory and the honor of the nations" is our daily work. New Testament scholar N. T. Wright elaborates,

> What you do in the Lord is not in vain. You are not oiling the wheels of a machine that's about to roll over a cliff. You are not restoring a great painting that's shortly going to be thrown on the fire. You are not planting roses in a garden that's about to be dug up for a building site. You are—strange though it may seem, almost hard to believe as the resurrection itself—accomplishing something that will become in due course part of God's new world. Every act of love, gratitude, and kindness; every work of art or music inspired by the love of God and delight in the beauty of his creation; every minute spent teaching a severely handicapped child to read or work; every act of care and nurture, of comfort and support for one's fellow human beings and for that matter one's fellow nonhuman creatures; and of course every prayer, all Spirit-led teaching, every deed that spreads the gospel, builds up the church, embraces and embodies holiness rather than corruption, and makes the name of Jesus honored in the world—*all of this will find its way, through the resurrecting power of God, into the new creation that God will one day make.*[1]

I hope you feel the weight and hope of this quote. Our work is not in vain; our work matters. Changing a diaper matters to God. Picking up garbage from the curb matters to God. Cleaning a toilet matters to God. Pounding nails with a hammer or with an electric nail gun matters to God. Preparing a meatloaf matters to God. Creating an Excel spreadsheet matters to God. Caring for an elderly parent matters to God. Editing a book matters to God. Filling a cavity in a patient's mouth matters to God. Teaching a Sunday School lesson matters to God. All these tasks are sacred tasks.

1. N. T. Wright, *Surprised by Hope,* 208.

Our society elevates some work as superior to other work. Some churches similarly elevate pastoral work and missionary work as more important than ordinary Monday through Friday work. But God does not have such a hierarchy. Wright's words are worth repeating when he says, "Every deed that spreads the gospel, builds up the church, embraces and embodies holiness rather than corruption, and makes the name of Jesus honored in the world—all of this will find its way, through the resurrecting power of God, into the new creation that God will one day make."

NOW WHAT?

If you are like me, Wright's outlook or vision sounds wonderful and so encouraging. However, what can we do now before we witness our work—through the resurrecting power of God—entering the new heavens and the new earth? We can follow my former seminary professor, Dr. Hans Bayer's admonition: "Live life now from the end of the story." What did he mean by this statement? Your knowledge of the end times should inform your daily work.

We know how the biblical story ends and what will be true of the new heavens and new earth. Work will be delightful and pleasurable. There will be no fraudulent bookkeeping, no shoddy work, no unethical work habits, no hiring discrimination, no secular/spiritual divide. Bring these realities into the present. As one colleague puts it, "Be a foretaste of heaven" in your workplace. To be a foretaste of heaven means simply to do good work. Do your work so well that it might qualify—through the resurrecting power of God—to make it into the new creation. Do your work so well that the community in heaven will pause and say, "Look, now that's good workmanship!" Other ways we can be a foretaste of heaven in the workplace include doing work that is above reproach, exposing corruption, and befriending someone who is being bullied (like Milton in the film *The Office*).

DISCUSSION QUESTIONS:

1. On a scale of 1 to 10, with 10 being good or excellent work, how would you rate your work?

2. How can you be an aroma of Christ on your job?

3. How can your work be a foretaste of heaven?

4. How can you live out Jesus' commandment, "love your neighbor as yourself" in the workplace?

5. How does N. T. Wright's quote inspire you to approach your work?

Bibliography

Bonk, Jon. *Missions and Money: Affluence as a Missionary Problem.* New Delhi: Intercultural Publications, 1996.

Bordewich, Fergus M. *Bound for Canaan: The Epic Story of the Underground Railroad, America's First Civil Rights Movement.* New York: Amistad, 2006.

Bridges, Jerry. *The Discipline of Grace: God's Role and Our Role in the Pursuit of Holiness.* Colorado Springs, CO: NavPress, 1994.

Cohen, Finkelstein, et al. Towards a Rabbinic philosophy of education. *The Samuel Friedland Lectures:* 1967–1974, 11–30.

Collis, Jack et al. The English Standard Version Study Bible. Wheaton, IL: Crossway, 2008.

Cornwall, Judson. *Things We Adore: How to Recognize and Get Free of Idolatry.* Shippensburg, PA: Destiny Image, 1991.

Crist, Terry M. *Learning the Language of Babylon: Changing the World by Engaging the Culture.* Grand Rapids, MI: Chosen, 2001.

Douglass, Frederick. *Oration In Memory Of Abraham Lincoln.* Delivered At The Unveiling Of The Freedmen's Monument In Memory Of Abraham Lincoln, In Lincoln Park, Washington, D.C., April 14, 1876. Online: http://american_almanac.tripod.com/dougorat.htm.

Driver, Plummer, et al. *The International Critical Commentary on the Holy Scriptures of the Old and New Testaments.* New York: C. Scribner's Sons, 1899.

Fogas, Jackie. "Student Profile: Shaping of a Shepherd." *Covenant Magazine* (2008), 24.

France, R.T., *Tyndale Commentary on Matthew,* Grand Rapids, MI: Eerdmans, 112.

Green, Michael. Evangelism in the Early Church. The Mount, Guildford, UK: Eagle, 1970.

Grigoriadis, Vanessa. "The Tragedy of Britney Spears: Rolling Stone's 2008 Cover Story." *Rolling Stone* (2008). Online: http://www.rollingstone.com/music/news/the-tragedy-of-britney-spears-rolling-stones-2008-cover-story-20110329.

Haack, Denis. "Walking on Christ's Property." *Critique* Magazine (2007), 2.

Hagner, Donald Alfred. *Matthew.* Dallas, TX: Word, 1995.

Bibliography

Kass, Leon R. "The Wisdom of Repugnance." *New Republic* 216 (1997), 17–26.

Lea, Thomas D., Jr., and Hayne P. Griffin, Jr. *The New American Commentary*. Nashville, TN: Broadman, 1991.

Lewis, C. S. *Mere Christianity*. New York: HarperOne, 2012.

Mattson, Ralph, and Arthur F. Miller. *Finding a Job You Can Love*. Nashville: Nelson, 1982.

McDowell, Sean. "True for You, but Not True for Me?" *Worldview Ministries* (2006). Online: http://www.seanmcdowell.org/index.php/youth-culture/ true-for-you-but-not-true-for-me/.

Mouw, Richard J. *Calvinism in the Las Vegas Airport: Making Connections in Today's World*. Grand Rapids, MI: Zondervan, 2004.

Nafukho, Fredrick Muyia. "Ubuntuism: An African Social Philosophy Relevant to Adult Learning and Workplace Learning." In *Comparative Adult Education Around the Globe*, edited by Kathleen King and Victor C. X. Wang, 63. Hangzhou, China: Zhejiang University Press, 2007.

Neuhaus, Richard J. "To Say Jesus Is Lord." *First Things* 107 (2000), 69–88.

Pearcey, Nancy. *Total Truth: Liberating Christianity from Its Cultural Captivity*. Wheaton, IL: Crossway, 2004.

Peterson, Eugene H. *The Contemplative Pastor*. Michigan: William B Eerdmans Pub., 1989.

Peterson, Eugene H. The Message Remix: The Bible in Contemporary Language. Colorado Springs, CO: Navpress, 2003.

Piper, John, Dr. "Let God Be True Though Every Man a Liar." *Desiring God*. Online: http://www.desiringgod.org/sermons/let-god-be-true-though- every-man-a-liar.

Plantinga, Cornelius. *Engaging God's World: A Christian Vision of Faith, Learning, and Living*. Grand Rapids, MI: W.B. Eerdmans, 2002.

Ryrie, Charles Caldwell. *Basic Theology*. Wheaton, IL: Victor, 1986.

Sullivan, Amy. "The Panera Model: How to Do Good and Make Money at the Same Time." National Journal (2013). Online: http://www.nationaljournal. com/next-economy/solutions-bank/the-panera-model-how-to-do-good- and-make-money-at-the-same-time-20130613.

Stevenson, Robert Louis. *The Strange Case of Dr. Jekyll and Mr. Hyde and Other Stories*. Pleasantville, NY: Reader's Digest Association, 1991.

Turner, Steve. *Imagine: A Vision for Christians in the Arts*. Downers Grove, IL: InterVarsity, 2001.

Veith, Gene Edward. God at Work: Your Christian Vocation in All of Life. Wheaton, IL: Crossway, 2011.

Wells, David F. *No Place for Truth, Or, Whatever Happened to Evangelical Theology?* Grand Rapids, MI: W.B. Eerdmans Pub., 1993.

Wolters, Albert M. *Creation Regained: A Transforming View of the World*. Leicester: Inter-Varsity, 1986.

Wright, N. T. Surprised by Hope: Rethinking Heaven, the Resurrection, and the Mission of God. New York, NY: HarperOne, 2008.

Young, William P. *The Shack: A Novel*. Newbury Park, CA: Windblown Media, 2007.

About the Author

Luke is director of resource and curriculum development for Made to Flourish (Overland Park, KS). Prior to joining Made to Flourish, Luke wrote curriculum for a marketplace ministry and served as Department Chair and Associate Professor for Christian Ministry Studies (CMS) at Lindenwood University in St. Charles, MO. He also served as Assistant Dean for Training Ministries at Covenant Theological Seminary (St. Louis, MO). In this capacity, Luke directed the Francis Schaeffer Institute, the Youth In Ministry Institute and oversaw the Field Education segments for the Master of Educational Ministries and Master of Divinity degrees. Prior to Covenant, Luke worked as an Electrical Engineer for 15 plus years.

Luke earned his PhD from the University of Missouri (St. Louis, MO); he also holds a Master of Divinity from Covenant Theological Seminary (St. Louis, MO) and B.S. and M.S. degrees in Electrical Engineering from the University of Kansas (Lawrence, KS) and University of Missouri (Columbia, MO), respectively.

His personal vision is to train Christians how to think Christianly about all of life and how to engage the culture winsomely and respectfully. He is married to Rita and they have two children—Briana and Caleb.